What About Cremation?

A CHRISTIAN PERSPECTIVE

John J. Davis

PINEGROVE
PUBLISHING

PO Box 557 • Winona Lake, IN 46590

Additional Publications by the Author

Books

Israel: From Conquest to Exile. A Commentary on Joshua through 2 Kings, 542 pages.

Paradise to Prison: Studies in Genesis, 363 pages.

Moses and the Gods of Egypt: Studies in Exodus. 350 pages.

Conquest and Crisis: Studies in Joshua, Judges and Ruth. 176 pages.

Biblical Numerology: A Basic Study of the Use of Numbers in the Bible. 174 pages.

The Birth of a Kingdom: Studies in 1 and 2 Samuel and 1 Kings 1-11. 209 pages.

The Mummies of Egypt. 143 pages.

What About Cremation? A Christian Perspective. 128 pages.

The Perfect Shepherd: Studies in the Twenty-third Psalm. 160 pages.

Contemporary Counterfeits: A Practical and Biblical Evaluation of Occultism. 43 pages.

Demons, Exorcism and the Evangelical. 16 pages

The Dead Sea Scrolls. 15 pages.

Real Fishermen Are Never Thin. 123 pages.

Real Fishermen Never Lie. 124 pages.

Real Fishermen Never Wear Suits. 121 pages.

Favorite Fish & Seafood Recipes. 223 pages.

A Lake Guide to Fishing and Boating in Kosciusko County, Indiana. 93 pages.

Chart

Hebrew Verb Chart: An Analysis of the Strong Verb.

Cassette Tape Sets

Conquest and Settlement, 12 Tapes and Syllabus (24 lectures)

The United Monarchy, 12 Tapes and Syllabus (24 lectures)

Video Cassette

Basics of Bass Fishing. A 35-minute color video.

To receive a complete free catalog, price list and ordering information, write: Pinegrove Publishing, P.O. Box 557, Winona Lake, IN 46590 or fax: 219-267-8875.

To

DR. HOMER A. KENT, JR.

in
appreciation for his friendship,
encouragement, and example of excellence
in biblical scholarship.

Published by: Pinegrove Publishing
P.O. Box 557
Winona Lake, IN 46590

FAX: 219-267-8875

Cover design by Kevin Carter.

ISBN 0-9635865-4-8

Table of Contents

Preface

Contemporary conversations rarely include the topics of death, dying, and burial. Emotionally this is understandable, but as one has put it, "Until one accepts the reality of death and thinks through the implications, he has not really accepted life."[1]

The rapid rise of the practice of cremation in the United States due to escalating funeral costs, a growing Asian population which long has utilized this custom for burial, major changes in position on this practice by the Roman Catholic Church, as well as other denominations, and a shortage of burial plots in some metropolitan areas has made this a topic of considerable interest.

Is cremation really a burial option for the Christian? What does the Bible have to say on this issue? Why has the Roman Catholic Church changed its position on this issue so dramatically?

These are but a few of the questions this writer has encountered in recent years while conducting seminars on this topic. Christians are asking probing questions on this issue and pastors are frustrated by the lack of helpful literature to put into their hands. Much of what has been written on cremation is highly passionate either for or against this practice.

This book has been written to meet a serious need in a fashion that is sensitive to biblical truth, accurate in its presentation of scientific data, and free from the highly emotional arguments that have clouded the whole issue.

The author is grateful to many who assisted in the production of this volume. Dr. Homer A. Kent, Jr., Dr. Larry Overstreet, and Mr. David L. Zapf all read the manuscript and offered valuable suggestions for improvement in both style and content. Special thanks goes to Jonathan Wiley who assisted with the research for this revised and expanded edition. It was with her usual skill and efficiency that Nancy Weimer assisted with the bibliography.

The photographs of cremation, as practiced in Singapore, were taken by Rev. James Lay Seng Chan with assistance from Rev. Philip Heng. I am most grateful for the generosity of these pastors in providing such unusual scenes. The excellent photos of urns, a modern oven, and a columbarium were taken by my father, John J. Davis, Sr. His assistance on, and encouragement for, the project are most appreciated.

Appreciation is also expressed to Akron Concrete Products, in Akron, Indiana for making it possible to photograph their crematory and the display of urns. The kind assistance of the folks at Lindenwood Cemetery in Fort Wayne, Indiana, resulted in the production of excellent photographs of both indoor and outdoor columbariums. Mr. Ned Titus, owner of Titus Funeral Home in Warsaw, Indiana, was also helpful in providing information on modern funeral practices and costs.

It is author's desire that this little volume will help to return the Christian funeral to an experience of simplicity, economy, dignity and spiritual significance.

Foreword

Cremation is causing Christians today to face many new questions about death. Indeed, the traditional American funeral with its rising costs has perhaps generated more discussion of cremation. Programs on television have added to this condition.

In my first years of pastoral experience, when a family faced the death of a loved one, cremation was never considered as a serious option. Recently, however, the topic of cremation is being examined as a more common alternative. Seminars are suggesting it, college and seminary students quiz their professor concerning it, pastors are more frequently confronted with questions regarding it, and family members and friends of a deceased individual are considering it.

Some discussions generate more "heat" than "light." However, Dr. John Davis has commendably provided needed light on this topic by answering pertinent questions: What are the issues involved? How should the subject be approached? When should cremation be seriously considered? What are the implications for the Christian faith? Which biblical passages and principles are applicable in dealing with this subject?

Anyone in pastoral ministry must face the subject of death, the funeral and all its attendant traditions, and the disposal of the body. Likewise, Christian families must prepare for the eventuality of death and make conscientious, God-honoring decisions concerning it.

As a pastor who has conducted scores of funerals, and as a seminary professor involved in the training of others for the ministry, I eagerly recommend this helpful volume by my colleague, Dr. Davis. Both the lay reader and the full time Christian worker will find this book helpful as it deals forthrightly and kindly with the issues involved with cremation.

What About Cremation? answers questions people have concerning cremation, bases its conclusions on the direct and implicit teaching of God's Word, and makes practical suggestions for making the Christian funeral more biblically centered and Christ glorifying. I believe this publication will both enlighten and encourage God's people to honor Him, even in death.

R. Larry Overstreet, Ph.D.

1 Introduction

Death is a difficult subject, but inescapable. Many will only discuss it with hushed tones, while others laugh it off casually as if it only represents a pothole in the journey of life.

In spite of valiant attempts by modern thanatologists, psychiatrists, and clinical specialists in parapsychology to shed significant light on this subject, death remains a dark mystery for most people. Modern thanatology has, for the most part, focused its efforts on experiential analysis and only deepened human uncertainty by conflicting evidence and sometimes bizarre stories by those who presumably had crossed the veil of death and returned.

The only sure word on this highly emotional and complex subject is to be found in Holy Scripture. God, who is man's creator and the One who instituted death as a judgment,[1] has provided man with significant insight into the nature of physical death and the afterlife. Only in the Bible can one find victory over the fear of death and, as a matter of fact, over death itself as the final experience that eternally separates the unrepentant sinner from his Maker.[2]

While the Scripture is very clear and comprehensive in its discussion of the spiritual and eternal aspects of death and how to prepare for that experience through personal faith in Jesus Christ, there is little either direct or indirect instruction as to the disposition of the body at the time of death.

The study of death and mortuary rituals is of significant value to both the biblical scholar and the anthropologist. Mortuary rituals consist of two fundamental components: the process of preparing the body and the burial site for deposition, and the rituals which accompany the funeral process. The yields of such study are of enormous value in understanding ancient cultures and peoples.[3]

What has become accepted custom among Christians has been established and perpetuated largely by cultural convenience or general biblical example. The Hebrews normally buried by simple interment or inhumation and this custom was strictly followed by Jesus and His followers.

In the long history of the Christian church, inhumation has been the normal burial tradition, but in recent days new questions have been raised by the growing popularity and economic attractiveness of cremation. Cremation is generally defined as that "mode of disposition in which the body of one who has died is quickly reduced by intense heat to its component elements."[4]

Unfortunately, the debate now raging over the acceptability or unacceptability of cremation as a burial option for the believer centers more on emotional issues rather than biblical ones.

For example, one writer who vigorously supports the practice of cremation characterizes inhumation as "body dumping"[5] and describes the results of interment as follows:

> People who once had enough money to build big and high monuments for themselves are usually the first to have the tops of their monuments fall to the ground—the cement holding the two sections together having dissolved with time. Worms will take care of the modern cemeteries that follow the practice of having their monument stones flush with the ground. Worms bring ground up to the surface when they come up to mate at night. Over a period of time the worms will bring up enough ground to cover the monument completely. Then the only way you will be able to be found is if, in some distant time, a building is built in the cemetery. Then the workmen can have their fun throwing your skull back and forth like a football as their tools break into one rotten coffin after another.[6]

Superficial arguments like the above or statements like, "Burial will be against the law by the year 2000. Given a choice between body dumping and cremation, Americans will choose cremation,"[7] are hardly responsible or helpful in this whole discussion.

Additionally, some advocates of inhumation have not been dispassionately objective in their presentations and this, too, is a disservice to the Christian public. One writer, for example, talks about cremation in the following manner:

> But to say it is aesthetic, could sound like the truth only to those who know nothing of the unpleasant and grotesque process of cremation. There is nothing really beautiful or graceful about any process of the disposal of a body, but this is less so when we revert to this modernized, heathen custom. How can one who knows of the twitching and jumping and noises that there are when the heat is turned on to 2,000 F. look upon the process as aesthetic? . . .
>
> . . . It is most revolting and repulsive to think of the body of a refined Christian being burnt to a crisp and finally to ashes.[8]

If this line of argument is to dominate the discussion, just think of the grotesque descriptions that could be produced of the process by which the body of one decays in the ground and what it must look like, say, after six months or one year. The chemical breakdown of the tissues, the activity of maggots and worms coupled with intrusion of rodents at later times does not exactly provide an aesthetically appealing picture.

If the Christian church is to come to grips with this issue, it must do so without emotionally charged characterizations of either inhumation or cremation. Indeed, the issue can only find acceptable resolution with a careful consideration of the history of crematory practice and its relationship to biblical and spiritual values.

Arguments of economy or profit have also been of questionable value in bringing this issue to a satisfactory resolution. The principal argument for cremation by many is the fact that it can be so much less expensive than embalming and interment. But, as will be shown below, this is not necessarily the case, because enterprising morticians can easily enrich the cost of cremation by a number of required auxiliary expenses. On the other hand, it is possible for inhumation to be carried out in a very economic fashion.

Sometimes the reluctance of funeral homes to encourage cremation is not out of aesthetic or theological concerns, but purely economic ones. While it is possible for the costs of cremation to be high as noted above, generally speaking, funeral homes do not realize the same level of profit from cremations as they do from embalming and interment. One writer observed the following:

> It is not surprising that there has always been a strong current
> of opposition to cremation among the undertakers, who are
> painfully aware of the financial hazards it presents to their end

of the funeral business. As one wrote, "Cremations in volume will ruin any funeral director's business. We cremate quite a few cases, and no matter how you figure it, we make a reasonable margin of profit on only about six percent of the caese we cremate."[9]

Very revealing is the fact that some funeral directors have openly admitted they have intimidated people into opting for inhumation by emotionally-charged descriptions of of the cremation process. A funeral director writing in *Mortuary Management* describes the approach.

> When anybody asks me about cremation, I simply tell them the truth: that it can be the cheapest way of disposing of a body, but that anyone who had ever witnessed a cremation wouldn't cremate a dog. I drop it right there, unless they ask me why I say that, and then I give them a blow-by-blow description of what happens in the retort. About four out of five back off immediately, and express no further interest in cremation![10]

Obviously, this subject, approached at any level, can be emotionally distorted. However, the purpose of this volume is to discuss the issue of cremation without resorting to emotional distortions and with honest and dispassionate evaluation of the facts.

The current discussions surrounding the issue of cremation have arisen largely due to the growing popularity of the practice since 1975 in the United States. In 1975 the corpses of only 7% of the deaths were handled by cremation, but by 1996 that figure had increased to 21.31%. The projection is that by the year 2010, 37.40% of all burials will be handled by cremation.[11]

Of course, these percentages are well below those of England and many other countries. In England, for example, more than 68% of all burials are by cremation, and this includes a large percentage of Christians.

In the United States, cremation is most frequently practiced on the west and east coasts. In California, for example, 88,770 individuals were cremated in 1996 which was 38.22% of all deaths. Florida was second 63,671 cremations or 41.41%, and New York third with 26,400 or 16.21%. California has 146 crematoriums while Florida has 107 and New York, 44. There are 1,181 crematoriums in the United States.[12] Internationally, based on 1994 figures, Japan had the most crematoriums with 1,942, followed by China with 1,288.

The trend in the western states (California, Arizona, Hawaii, Oregon and Washington) as well as Alaska, is clearly toward more cremations. In 1986, 48.91% of all burials in Hawaii were by cremation, but by 1996 that figure had jumped to 58.25%. The same type of trend is seen in Alaska where the figures are 32.51% and 54.96% respectively.[13]

Eastern states are exhibiting the same trends. Maine, for example, had 19.12% of its burials by cremation in 1986, and that number had escalated to 39.75% in 1996. In New Jersey, the numbers were 18.11% and 25.17% respectively. Massachusetts went from 13.45% in 1986 to 22.45% in 1996 while New Hampshire went from 18.91% to 35.36% in the same time period.[14]

In certain cities, the rate of cremations to deaths is very high. Oakland, California recorded 16,419 cremations which was 67.2% of all deaths. The Tampa Bay area had 22,704 deaths with 45.5% buried by cremation.[15]

In 1992, 70,000 Canadians were cremated, more than one third of the total who died in that year and 10,000 more than in 1989.

There are now close to 100 varieties of urns on the market, costing as little as $20 for a plastic one to as much as $3,500 for a 24K-goldplated model encrusted with sapphires.

According to researchers, there are at least six trends that are affecting the growth of cremation in the United States: (1) Society is becoming middle aged, (2) Educational level is rising, (3) The earnings gap is widening, (4) Origins of immigrants are changing, (5) People and jobs are spreading outward and (6) Regional differences are diminishing.[16]

The scattering of families to geographically distant areas has been a significant factor in the rising popularity of cremation. Costs for transporting a body from Europe to the United States exceed $2500 while the journey from Asia can go as high as $4500. While transportation of a body is considerably less within the United States, it nonetheless is a good deal more than the transportation of cremains (the term used of cremated remains).

The secularization of American society is also having its impact on funeral and burial traditions. Certain traditional values attached to the body and the funerary process have been largely neglected by a society that is less and less influenced by churches or synagogues.

Should cremation be considered an acceptable mortuary practice for Christians? To answer this question, the practice of cremation from ancient to modern times is examined. Next, biblical data that relate to crematory acts are discussed. The final chapter of this volume is devoted to conclusions and suggestions for modern funeral practices. It is important that, whatever conclusions are reached on this difficult subject, they are biblically supported, socially acceptable, and emotionally helpful.

The discussions in this book are directed primarily to those who take Scripture seriously and are willing to be influenced by its truth.

2

Historical Perspective

Funerary rituals and disposal of the body of the deceased has always been a matter of social and religious importance. In many cases, burial method was reflective of religious notion and tribal tradition.

While much has been written over the years on early burial rites and practices, it has not been until recent decades that archaeology has provided the materials necessary to verify many of the details.

Ancient burial practices and the assemblages placed with the deceased have long fascinated the modern mind and have been the object of intensive study. The practice of inhumation has been well documented in most cultures, but burials involving cremated remains have been more elusive.

Happily, modern archaeological technique with its emphasis on disciplined stratigraphic analysis has given more attention to the subtleties of soil change and the presence of ash materials, thus providing for a better understanding of the early practices of cremation.

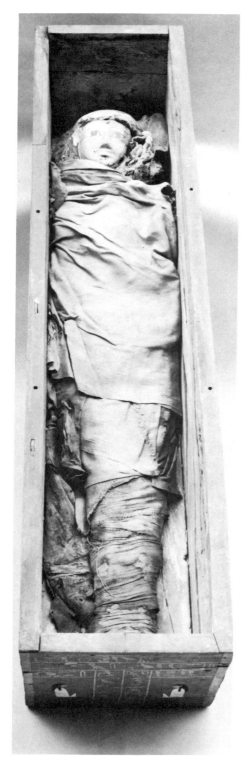

New-born child found in Tarkhan (Roman Period). There is no evidence of disease. *Courtesy the British Museum.*

The remains of a middle-aged man named Ankhef from the XI Dynasty. Studies have shown he suffered from osteoarthritis of the spine and the left hip. *Courtesy the British Museum.*

A number of issues arise when the general subject of burial practice is examined and any discussion of cremation, whether ancient or modern, must address them. For example, why were people cremated in ancient times? What does it tell us regarding their understanding of the meaning of death and the afterlife? What benefits did it have (if any) for the family and other mourners? While archaeological discovery can help us with some of these issues, others will be subject to some speculation.

I. PREHISTORIC PRACTICE OF CREMATION

All early evidence seems to indicate that simple interment of the corpse was the earliest form of burial practice. When and for what reasons cremation began to be practiced is still shrouded in some measure of mystery.

There seems to be some consensus that the earliest cremations are to be traced to the Stone Ages in both Europe and the Near East.[1] E. O. James suggests that the earliest cremations may well have been accidental.[2] Fire has been long associated with burial practices through, for example, the lighting of fires at the graves of the dead and through the offering of burnt animal sacrifices. Possibly, the transition from inhumation to cremation was influenced by these traditions,[3] or the body could have been accidentally burned by such funerary fires.[4]

Evidence exists for cremation in Neolithic times in Palestine, Syria, the Peloponnese, Germany and Hungary.[5] Pottery vessels have been discovered containing the ash remains of one or more persons in the Neolithic graves of Bohemia, Moravia, central Germany, Hungary and England.[6] In some instances of prehistoric cremations, the bones had to be broken up after incineration. Such bones were simply crushed with a stone after they had cooled in order to fit them into a burial container or make them easier to transport.[7]

The bone remains of a Roman inhumation in the 2nd cent. A.D. This unexcavated loculus was located in Abila Tomb H-2. *Photo by John J. Davis.*

An unexcavated burial chamber in a Roman Tomb at Abila in Jordan. Earlier burials have been pushed to the rear to make room for the latest inhumation. *Photo by the Author.*

Not all early cremations were poorly executed, however. After a series of comparisons with present day cremations and a number of experiments with the reburning of prehistoric samples of pulverized bone, Nils-Gustaf Gejvall concluded that he had "become convinced that cremating technologies in pre-historic times must have gained a very high level of efficiency."[8]

However, while archaeological evidence documents the early practice of cremation, at no time did it become the dominant custom of burial except for short periods in Britain and North and East-central Europe.[9]

II. CREMATION IN THE ANCIENT WORLD

Various reasons have been given for the development of cremation among peoples of the ancient Near East. It has been suggested that burning the body was an offering to the gods[10] or to set the soul free.[11] Others have suggested that cremation was practiced because it was less expensive than inhumation,[12] it prevented the spread of disease, or because it made room for more burials in a tomb.[13]

Evidence of human cremation has been discovered at ancient Sardis,[14] Carchemish,[15] Azbr (11th cent. B.C.), Tell Fara (south, 9th cent. B.C.), Tell Ajjul (9th cent. B.C.), and Tell er-Reqeish (850 B.C.) in Palestine, and a number of sites in Phoenicia.[16]

A text from Nuzi (XII:165) seems to refer to a royal cremation with the line, "at the time when the king Surattarna died and was cremated." E. Gaal, however, maintains that it was funerary objects that were burned and not the king.[17] Archaeological evidence exists which indicates that a few of the Hittite kings had been cremated.[18]

It has frequently been argued that Semitic peoples never practiced cremation and when such practices appear at Semitic sites, it represents the presence of foreigners. While this may be generally true, evidence of cremation prior to the arrival of the "Sea Peoples" (1200 B.C.) at Alaalakh might indicate that some Semites had adopted the practice[19] just as the Hebrews adopted pagan practices of human sacrifice during times of spiritual apostasy.

The normal practice for the Hebrews, however, was inhumation and if cremation was utilized, it either represented a departure from accepted practice or was necessary because of special circumstances. As Roland deVaux has observed, to "burn a body was an outrage, inflicted only upon notorious criminals (Gen. 38:24; Lev. 20:14; 21:9), or upon enemies a man wanted to annihilate forever (Amos 2:1)."[20] More detailed discussion of Hebrew thought and practice regarding death and burial will follow in Chapter 4.

A. Greece

The Greeks believed that death and the resultant dissolution of the body provided the means for the emancipation of the soul. Fire was regarded as a purifying agent and aided in the release of the soul after death. Mythology saw the burning of the body as a means to unify the body with its original elements.[21]

The introduction of cremation to the Greek mainland seems to have been a gradual process, but it never completely replaced the earlier elaborate Mycenean inhumations. Evidence indicates that the practice of cremation entered ancient Greece about 1000 B.C. from the north. At Argos, Perati, in the Athenian Kerameikos and on the island of Salamis some cremation was practiced along with inhumation without any apparent distinction in funerary rites.[22]

Cremation was utilized frequently by the Greek army fighting in foreign lands so that the remains of the dead could be transported more easily to their homeland. It was also a means by which desecration of the body by the enemy could be prevented. Such a practice also aided in the prevention of disease, which might accompany handling of corpses in various stages of decay.

Of special interest is the fact that the right to be cremated was denied to suicides, infants who did not possess teeth and individuals who had been struck by lightning which was assumed to result from a special judgment of the gods. It is clear from these exclusions that cremation was understood to have a different effect on the dead than simple inhumation.[23]

Excavations in a cemetery at Neo Ionia near Athens revealed that the standard burial method for children was inhumation, but for adults cremation was adopted.[24]

B. *Rome*

According to most scholars, cremation was practiced in Rome as early as the eighth century B.C. This judgment is supported by archaeological evidence. The Sepulcretum in the Roman Forum, which dates from the eighth to the sixth century B.C., contains both cremations and inhumations.[25] That cremation was a widespread practice in the fifth century B.C. is demonstrated in the Law of the Twelve Tablets.[26]

From about 400 B.C. until A.D. 200 cremation was a very common form of burial in Rome, although interment continued to be practiced. This has not only been well documented in excavations in Italy, but in outlying provinces as well. Evidence of cremation in Jordan during the first century B.C. was found in Heshbon Tomb F.31. Resting on disarticulated bone material in Loculus 1 was a unique four-handled cooking pot which contained the ash remains of a cremation.[27]

Like the Greeks, the Romans forbade the cremation

Roman Tomb F.31 at Heshbon in Jordan. Note the various loculi around the central chamber which was typical of Roman tombs of the period. *Photo by the Author.*

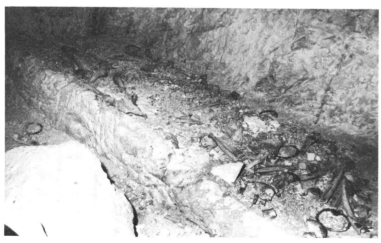

Two disturbed burials in a Late Roman tomb at Abila in Jordan. Iron rings which were part of the bier used to carry the body can be seen on the bench and floor. *Photo by the Author.*

A Roman Columbarium at el-Jib (Gibeon). *Photo by the Author.*

of anyone who had been killed by lightning. "It is not improbable that this prohibition might originate from the idea, that such persons had been already purified, or consecrated by the stroke of fire from heaven." [28] As noted above, however, it is also possible that cremation was denied the corpse in these cases because the death was regarded as a judgment, and purification of the soul by the cremation fires would be impossible.

Cremation in the Roman Empire was popular until it began to decline around A.D. 200. It was officially forbidden during the reign of Constantine the Great (A.D. 306-337). [29] Why the practice waned after the second century A.D. has been the subject of considerable speculation. Some have argued that the rise of Christianity brought about this change, [30] but since the practice declined in areas not influenced by Christianity, this may provide only a partial explanation. Other religious influences may have been at work as well.

It has been suggested that the decline was due to changes in fashion. "By fashion we mean the habits of

Cremated remains of an Early Roman burial in Heshbon Tomb F.31. These ash remains had been placed in a clay cooking pot. *Photo by the Author.*

the rich, which gradually permeated the classes below them. Burial seems to have made its appeal to them because it presented itself in the form of the use of the sarcopha gus. This was expensive and gratified the instinct for ostentation."[31]

Whatever the precise reason for this change, most agree that it represented a new respect for the individual and a means by which they could lay "to rest the mortal frame which has been the temple and mirror of the immortal soul and enduring personality."[32]

C. Europe

The practice of cremation in both western and eastern Europe is well documented back to the Middle Bronze Age (*c.* 1800 B.C.). It began in Scandinavia during the

Middle Bronze Age and grew slowly but with "startling thoroughness" from Indo-European areas northward through Germany.[33] As in Greece, it was commonly believed that fire freed the spirit for its journey in the after life.

Cremation was especially popular among those of high station in life and among the Vikings. During the Viking age it was fashionable to cremate important sailors in a ship. "The dead man rests on a bed within the ship surrounded by all the necessities of life and many choice possessions with various animals sacrificed to accompany him, and the dead slave girl laid in a tent beside him."[34]

According to Norse mythology, harmful spirits of the dead would plague the living after an improper burial. Cremation was necessary, therefore, to prevent this from occurring.[35]

Archaeology indicates that Anglo-Saxons practiced both inhumation and cremation throughout most of their history. Ashes from a cremation were normally buried in a specially prepared container while a corpse was placed in a grave with grave goods. According to Gale Owen, "cremation was more popular in Anglian areas while inhumation in Saxon areas and in Kent."[36]

Excavations at a number of sites have indicated that once the funeral fire had died down, the remains of the body, sacrifice (if any), and grave goods were collected, often incompletely burned. The burnt bones would normally be broken or crushed by the collapse of the pyre, but large pieces would remain. These would be broken so they could fit into a proper burial container. "The practice here seems to have been irregular, sometimes careless."[37]

In Poland cremation is attested back to at least 1300 B.C. and continued into the Middle Ages. "From 1300 to 300 B.C. cremation became an almost universal practice and extended far beyond the boundaries of modern Po-

The unexcavated interior of Loculus 1 in Heshbon Tomb F.31. This burial chamber contained several inhumations and the ash remains of a cremation were found in the cooking pot (right center of the photo). This Roman tomb dated to the first century A.D. *Photo by the Author.*

land." [38] Inhumation continued to be practiced during all this time but only to a limited degree.

During the twelfth and thirteenth centuries A.D., there appeared in Catholic Europe the somewhat gruesome custom of boiling the body of the deceased in water to facilitate the separation of the flesh from the bones. This practice developed as a means of bringing home more easily the remains of a wealthy prince or nobleman who had died in a distant land.

This macabre practice was ended, however, by Pope Boniface VIII in 1288 under penalty of excommunication and refusal of burial with Church rites. [39]

D. *Asia*

Cremation was first practiced extensively in India as early as the middle of the second millennium B.C., and it is assumed to have been introduced, along with Hinduism, by the Aryan invasion. [40] Buddha was cremated in India about 483 B.C. and the spread of Buddhism carried the custom to much of eastern Asia, including Indochina, Japan, and Korea. [41] Common mythology taught that fire resolved the body into its basic elements of fire, water, earth, and air. Many sects also believed that cremation prevented the spirit of evil people from returning to taunt the living.

There were exceptions to the common practice of cremation in India, however. Children who died were usually buried at the threshold of their home with the belief that they would be reborn to begin life again. This belief has been linked with the idea that burial made it possible for the child to return to the womb of Earth Mother. [42]

A notable exception to this burial tradition in eastern Asia was ancient China where inhumation seems to have been practiced consistently except when foreign domination was involved. [43]

E. North and South America

Cremation was practiced by the North American Indians, but it was usually reserved for individuals of special importance.[44] The Indians of central California are known to have cremated their dead.[45] In addition to primary cremations, there is archaeological evidence for some practice of secondary cremation in early Massachusetts sites. These burials were characterized by the use of red ocher and the placement of simple grave furnishings.[46]

In South America, the practice of cremation was most common to cultures north of the Amazon River. It was introduced to Central America by the Aztecs who burned the bodies of those who died by accident, sickness, or old age. When the cremation was completed, the ashes were placed in a vase along with a small jewel "heart" and the vase was then buried.[47]

F. Cremation and The Early Church

For the most part, the early church practiced inhumation and rigorously opposed cremation. Prompt burials followed death and a special memorial service was conducted the third day following the believer's death. The choice of the third day was a means of reaffirming belief in the resurrection of Jesus Christ and the ultimate resurrection of all believers.

Tertullian took delight in ridiculing the pagan practice of cremation because he saw startling inconsistencies in employing fire to dispose of the corpse and then using fire to offer sacrifices to the dead. He argued as follows:

> But I will deride the ordinary lot of mankind, especially when it cremates the dead most cruelly and afterwards feeds them most gluttonously, thereby propitiating them and offending them by one and the same fire. O piety that amuses itself with cruelty! Is

it sacrifice or insult which it offers when it burns its offering to
those already burnt?[48]

Christians normally buried the deceased in a simple
shroud utilizing wooden or sometimes lead coffins. One
exception to this was the Coptic practice in Egypt of
mummifying the dead.

The overwhelming consensus of early church writers
and leaders was that cremation was associated with rites
that were incompatible with many basic tenets of their
faith. In an effort to frustrate the faith of early Christians
in the resurrection, persecutors of the church had the
bodies of martyrs burned and their ashes scattered in the
wind or on a river.

So deep was the conviction of the early church on
this matter, that when a barbarian was converted to
Christianity, he was required to give up the practice of
cremation and bury by simple interment.[49]

G. *Summary*

Cremation, as has been observed above, was both
early in origin and widespread in geographic scope. For
the most part, it was associated with pagan ideas about
the essence of life or mythical beliefs regarding the
afterlife.

3

Modern Practices
of Cremation

Whether one lives in a culturally primitive land or a high-tech western country, death requires the disposal of the corpse, the emotional reorientation of the bereaved and the readjustment of the survivors to changed environments and relationships.

In the disposition of the corpse, cremation is widely practiced around the world. The end result of the process is always basically the same, namely, the reduction of the body to ash and bone fragments, but the rituals and the interpretation of the process differ widely.

I. PRACTICES AROUND THE WORLD

A. *Europe*

Until the year 1889, cremation was illegal in France. After that date it was permitted, but only if two doctors had viewed the corpse before incineration and provided authorities with a certificate of death.[1] Today any person of any age may choose either cremation or inhumation and the instructions provided by the person before his or her death are legally binding. In fact, executors who do not comply with such wishes are liable to a considerable fine.[2] Even though the practice of cremation is legal in France, few employ it. The common form of burial is inhumation without embalming and this cost as little as $100 in 1970.[3]

The first crematory in Germany was constructed in 1878 at Gotha.[4] Today both inhumation and cremation are employed, but in many locations where inhumation is practiced, the bodies are removed after 30 years. A simple coffin burial usually costs about $400.[5]

Cremation was practiced in England in isolated locales, but the formation of the Cremation Society in 1874 brought the whole issue to the forefront. As controversy raged both in and out of the church, the government declared cremation to be illegal in 1879. But the decision was reversed and cremation was legalized in 1884. Since then it has enjoyed growing popularity, especially since it is accepted by most churches in the land.[6] Today about 70 percent of all burials in Great Britain utilize cremation.[7]

According to English law, a person ceases to have any legal control of his body at the moment of death. If there are particular desires with regard to the type of burial, special provisions must be made to assure that this wish will be honored.

Conventional wisdom states that, if one desires cremation or inhumation, the best way to guarantee this is to leave property to the one responsible for the disposal of the body but to make receiving the property contingent on fulfilling the desires of the deceased.[8]

The late Sir Benjamin Richardson, an early advocate of cremation in modern England, relates the following story, which nicely illustrates the point.

An old gentleman called on Sir Benjamin one day. He stated that he had been so much impressed by what he read on the subject that he most earnestly desired that his body should be cremated at his death, but his family would not hear of such a thing.

In these circumstances he begged Sir Benjamin to consent to act as executor in order that his wishes might be carried out. Sir Benjamin explained the legal position, and suggested his visitor leave a large sum of money to the cremation society in the event of objections being raised by his daughter, who would otherwise receive his fortune.

Shortly after this interview the old gentleman died. Almost immediately Sir Benjamin received a visit from a clergyman, who said he had heard of his father-in-law's peculiar desire to be cremated, but he was sorry to say he could not allow this to take place as both he and his wife held very strong views on the subject.

Sir Benjamin Richardson observed, "that of course if it was really against the wishes of the family he could do nothing to prevent them disposing of the body by burial, but," he added, "as a matter of fact, I'm jolly glad, for in that case my society will benefit to the extent of something like ten thousand pounds." This unexpected announcement produced the desired effect.

On the following day Sir Benjamin received a letter from the clergyman, who wrote that after due consideration, the family had decided that as it would be a greater sin to allow the money to go to the society, they withdrew all opposition to the cremation of their relative's remains.[9]

One of the principal arguments of the cremation movement in England is the scarcity of land. Widespread support from the wealthy and the medical profession have also aided in its wide acceptance.[10] Cremated remains are either buried or, as is more popular, scattered in a special garden area of a cemetery or even in one's private yard. Today, about 90% of all cremated remains are scattered or "strewn" as ministers commonly refer to it.

Ashes of the deceased can be scattered over the ocean or from a plane over the countryside, but the popular preference is for the remains to be scattered in a "Garden of Remembrance." Such gardens are located in most cemeteries.[11]

While cremation is still not widely practiced in Italy, it does have a long history. The first serious experiments in modern cremation techniques were carried out by Brunetti in Italy in the year 1869. His furnace, which bore his name, was placed on public exhibit in Vienna in 1873.[12] The influence of the Roman Catholic Church prevented widespread adoption of the practice, but it is on the increase since the church relaxed its stand against cremation.

In a number of European countries like West Germany, Greece, Portugal, Sweden, and Spain, when a body is interred in the ground, it is sometimes removed later for a secondary, less space-consuming burial.[13]

All male bands frequently are present at Chinese funerals in Singapore. The more noise, the better according to tradition because it scares away evil spirits. *Photo by Rev. James Lay Seng Chan.*

An Urn Storage Area in a Crematorium in Singapore. *Photo by Rev. James Lay Seng Chan.*

B. *The Far East*

While cremation was prohibited in Japan in 1875,[14] it is practiced by more than 80% of the population today.[15] There are more than 4400 crematories scattered throughout the country, and in 1968, more than 621,000 bodies were cremated.[16]

On the day after the cremation of a family member, a surviving relative goes to the crematory to perform the "honorable bone-gathering" duty. He receives the ash and bone remains and about a week later either deposits them in a temple or buries them in a family cemetery plot. Tombstones are commonly utilized to mark the burial in the family cemetery.[17] In Thailand it is the practice to preserve the body for a short time by embalming and then cremate it with elaborate ritual. In the case of royalty, it is not unusual for the body to be

Rev. Philip Heng points to the firing chamber of a modern crematory oven in Singapore. *Photo by Rev. James Lay Seng Chan.*

The firing chamber of a crematory oven in Singapore. *Photo by Rev. James Lay Seng Chan.*

A Chinese urn with gifts. *Photo by Rev. James Lay Seng Chan.*

An elaborately decorated Chinese urn. *Photo by Rev. James Lay Seng Chan.*

An elaborate ceramic urn used in Chinese cremations. It is common for a photograph of the deceased to be placed on the front of the urn. The joss sticks in the lower right hand corner are burned for a period of 49 days. *Photo by Rev. James Lay Seng Chan.*

preserved in state for as long as six months to a year before cremation is carried out.[18]

Chinese occupants of Singapore, who are committed to Buddhism and other eastern religions, normally practice cremation while Christians generally bury the body. Ancestor worship remains strong in Singapore as it does in China and Hong Kong. One of the important times of the year for many families in Singapore is the *Qingming* festival when relatives of the deceased bring food and other gifts to the grave.

Today it not unusual to see at the graves miniature

Offerings for the dead are common in Singapore. Here a car and house are made of paper and bamboo. These will be burned with the belief that they will be transferred to the netherworld for the benefit of the deceased. *Photo by Rev. James Lay Seng Chan.*

Inside view of the paper automobile complete with driver and fake money. The money is often referred to as "hell currency." *Photo by Rev. James Lay Seng Chan.*

television sets, cars, stereos, and other material goods made of paper.[19] The *Qingming* festival is observed by the Chinese as a time to visit the graves of ancestors for the purpose of honoring the dead, and it also provides an opportunity for families to reunite. "Although remembrance rites are not as lavish as in the past, when professional wailers cried to the shrill dirges of monks and their pipes and cymbals, offerings to the dead are still extravagant."[20]

Cremation is widely practiced in India, but inhumation continues to be preferred by some tribes and Christian churches. Other burial customs are also followed such as exposing the bodies of the deceased on a platform where the flesh is plucked off by birds. The bones are then gathered up and placed in an ossuary.[21] Among the Mohammedan tribes, inhumation is practiced with the body usually being interred within 24 hours of death.

A unique feature of Tibetan cremation is the collection and grinding of the bone fragments into ash. The ash is then cast into medallions, which are placed in suitable niches as memorials.[22]

A view of a coffin and body just 15 minutes into the cremation process. *Photo by Rev. James Lay Seng Chan.*

II. THE UNITED STATES

A. *Some Early Practices*

The first recorded cremation in the United States took place in 1792 when Colonel Henry Laurens, who was a member of Washington's military staff and president of the Continental Congress of 1777 and 1778, was cremated on his own estate in Charleston, South Carolina.[23]

His will read as follows:

> I solemnly enjoin it upon my son as an indispensable duty that, as soon as he conveniently can after my decease, he cause my

body to be wrapped in twelve yards of tow cloth, and burnt until it is entirely consumed, and then, collecting my ashes, deposit them wherever he may see proper.[24]

He chose this method of burial because he was deeply afraid of being buried alive. One of his daughters was nearly buried in such a manner, and he was continually plagued by this prospect. Interestingly, the Catholic church recognizes this fear as one of several acceptable reasons for selecting cremation.[25]

The first crematory in the United States was built by Dr. F. J. LeMoyne on his own property in Washington, Pennsylvania, in 1876 for his personal use. LeMoyne, a medical doctor, had left the Christian church over the issue of abolition. Others, however, also utilized the facility in the years that followed. One of these was a member of the newly-formed Theosophical Society of New York. By the year 1884, there were 41 recorded cremations in the United States.[26]

Ash and bone remains of a modern cremation before processing. *Photo by Rev. James Lay Seng Chan.*

A refrigeration unit used to store the body until cremation. Some states and provinces in Canada have a mandatory waiting period of 24 or 48 hours before the remains can be burned. *Photo by John J. Davis, Sr.*

Today there are 960 crematories the United States and 107 in Canada.[27] Laws that restricted the deposit of cremains to cemeteries in the past have been rescinded by most states. Only Indiana prohibits the scattering of ashes. Scattering of the ashes is often seen as "a reunion with the natural world."[28] The cremains can also be placed in a columbarium or interred in an "urn garden" with a special marker, as is common in traditional interments.

B. *Cremation Societies*

Between 1881 and 1885 a number of cremation societies were organized throughout the United States, and they continue to function today. These societies provide information services and assist in making cremation arrangements. One of the largest, with more than 250,000 members, is the Neptune Society.[29]

Some societies, such as the Telophase Society based in San Diego, have created a stir with the promotion

A modern crematory oven located in Akron, Indiana. *Photo by John J. Davis, Sr.*

A modern crushing or processing machine. Large bone fragments enter from the top left, are processed and are collected in the metal drawer at the bottom. *Photo by John J. Davis, Sr.*

of inexpensive cremation arrangements ($250 to $600). Founded in 1971 by Dr. Thomas Weber, a biochemist and immunologist, the society requires a membership fee. When death occurs, the body is cremated and the ashes scattered at sea.[30] There are more than 30 such cremation clubs in California today.

The Telophase Society in Stamford, New York, charged about $600 in 1983 for its services.[31] There were no funeral directors, wakes, coffins, or limousines involved with this service. The society assists the family in planning for a memorial service if it is desired.[32]

The Cremation Association of America, located in Chicago, provides information and assistance for cremation societies, cemeterians, and funeral directors. The Association, which was founded in 1913, is very active in the publication of literature and organizes technical and educational seminars as well as public relations programs.

C. *The Growth of Cremation*

Cremation has seen its most rapid growth among the white, upper middle class in the United States. Inhumation is still generally practiced among the poor and uneducated as well as the white middle class.[33] California and Florida, with their large populations of retired people on fixed income, have exhibited the most dramatic increases in the practice of cremation.

Florida, for example, recorded 43,198 cremations in 1988, while the entire southeast region had 41,328 in 1982.[34] California had 79,627 cremations in 1988, and it is projected that the number will increase to 116,598 in the year 2000.[35]

Perhaps the most significant indicator of change in burial practices in the United States has been the appearance of "memorial gardens" in church cemeteries for the deposit of cremains. Clearly this provision by mainline

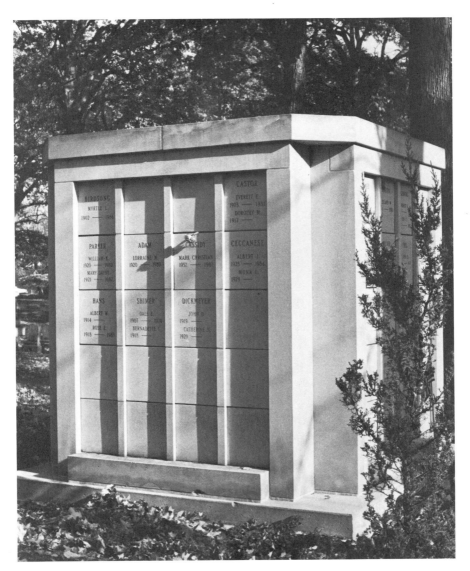

Exterior of a modern columbarium located at Lindenwood Cemetery in Fort Wayne, Indiana. Names of the deceased appear on the outside of the actual burial unit. *Photo by John J. Davis, Sr.*

A chapel at Lindenwood Cemetery where services may be held either before or after the cremation. *Photo by John J. Davis, Sr.*

denominational churches has aided the acceptance of cremation on the part of the religious public.

Another interesting trend in the United States is the desire to have animals, most notably pets, cremated. This is not a new notion because some ancient peoples cremated animals to make peace with a natural force that they perceived to be in the process of destroying them.[36]

Modern pet cremation usually costs about $125 including an urn. Most cremains of pets are buried, but some people keep the cremains their homes in elaborate urns.

D. *Burial Methods*

Actually, there are a number of burial methods practiced in North America. In one of the more exotic methods, known as "cryogenic interment," the body is placed in a capsule containing liquid nitrogen cooled to 320 degrees below zero immediately after death. The assumption is that sometime in the future medical science may develop a method of reviving these bodies and thereby restore life to the individual.

Coking is a method of burial by which the body is exposed to a flameless heat and reduced to a hard, brittle substance instead of ashes. Another form of burial involves the electro-plating process, that is, the application of a perfectly even metallic coating to the surface of the body by the same process that produces the electrotype plate. What, in effect, is produced is a statue that preserves even the expression on the individual's face. "To this process there would seem to be no valid objection," states an article in the *Telegraph* of 1887. "No change is brought about in appearance, except that face and figure are covered with a shining veil, through which the familiar lineaments appear with their well remembered characteristics and expression," the article concludes.[37]

Among the heat oriented processes, however, cremation remains the most widely practiced. This method basically brings about a rapid oxidation of the body tissues though intense heat. Under favorable cremating conditions the water in the body is evaporated, the carbon-containing tissues are completely burned, and the inorganic ash of the body framework, amounting to about five to seven pounds, is all that remains.[38] In order to

A modern columbarium at the Lindenwood Cemetery in Fort Wayne, Indiana. *Photo by John J. Davis, Sr.*

produce efficient incineration without smoke, temperature within the cremation chamber needs to be at least 2000 degrees Fahrenheit.

In most modern ovens, the heat is supplied by either gas, oil, or electricity. Gas, which was first used in Milan in 1876, is preferred because it is less expensive and permits greater control of the heat. The fuel is usually turned off ten minutes after the cremation has started and only the combustion air is left on. The fuel is not turned on again until after the casket has been consumed.

After the burning has been completed, a powerful fan is used to blow away the true ash. A magnet extracts metal pieces such as nails, fittings, etc. from the bone remains, and a crusher then reduces the bones (mistakenly called the ashes today) to pieces that generally measure one to two centimeters.[39] Generally, the total time required for a cremation is one and one half to two hours.

E. *Trends Among Religious Organizations*

Perhaps the most dramatic change with regard to the practice of cremation has occurred within the Roman

Typical urns utilized throughout the United States. *Photo by John J. Davis, Sr.*

Catholic Church. Early papal edicts forbade cremation and considered those who practiced it to be enemies of the church. When cremation societies began to appear in Europe in the 19th century, the church, in a May 19, 1886, edict, forbade Roman Catholics to join those societies or to have their bodies cremated.[40] This strong stance was taken largely because the proponents of cremation were either materialists or opponents of the church and its doctrines.

The edict stood until July 5, 1963, when an Instruction from the Vatican removed the penalties that were placed on Roman Catholics who were cremated.[41]

The change was brought about because the reasons individuals used for cremation were space, economics, war, and hygiene—none of which were focused on denying the doctrines of the church. In 1966 the Vatican relaxed the rule that prevented priests in England and Wales from conducting services at a crematorium, and this concession has now been extended to the entire Roman Catholic Church.[42] Individuals are no longer required to seek permission from church authorities before choosing cremation. However, a priest is not permitted to officiate if the individual chose cremation as a challenge to the Catholic faith.

While the Roman Catholic Church still encourages burial by inhumation, it does acknowledge private and public issues that may warrant cremation. Examples of private issues are a fear of being buried alive, an instinctive horror of being buried in the earth, a vivid imagination about the slow process of decomposition in the grave, or any other reason that is not in conflict with Catholic teaching.[43] Public reasons include ecological concerns or the results of war. In this connection, it should be observed that the Roman Catholic Church has always permitted cremation under certain circumstances, even before the Instruction of 1963.[44]

Two of the furnaces at Dachau, Germany, where thousands of Jews were cremated before and during World War II. Many Jews feel that the cremation of their body is inapproprite in the light of the horrors that took place in locations like Dachau and Auschwitz. *Photo by Jonathan Wiley.*

In some cases, due to state law regarding cremation, the Roman Catholic Church has had to adapt its funeral rites to the practice of cremation as Father Leo Steinback has done on the Japanese island of Honshu.[45]

Among protestant denominations, the situation regarding the practice of cremation varies. Mainline and generally liberal groups tend to accept the practice, but conservative organizations either reject it or discourage it. The Church of Jesus Christ of Latter Day Saints (Mormon) discourages it, but does not forbid it. Jehovah's Witnesses are admonished to "consider local legal requirements as well as the sentiments of those in the community in deciding on this matter (Phil. 1:10). Since

Jehovah does not express disapproval of cremation in the Bible, it remains a matter for personal decision."[46]

Unitarian-universalists fully approve of cremation and often prefer it. The practice is common among Buddhists, Hindus, and followers of Hare Krishna.[47]

Religious groups that strongly oppose or forbid the cremation of corpses are Moslems, Eastern Orthodox Churches, and some segments of the Jewish community (see below).

F. *Trends in the Jewish Community*

The historic position of Orthodox Judaism is that cremation is not an acceptable mode of burial. The principal text used in defense of this position is Deut. 21:23a, which reads, "His body shall not remain all night upon the tree, but thou shalt in any wise bury him that day." This passage, along with similar ones,[48] is regarded as a positive command.

"Rabbinical law prohibits cremation (Jer. *Kethubot* 11:1). Cremation is deemed disrespectful to the deceased, and is also regarded as a denial of the principle of resurrection."[49] In fact, the Talmud regards the act of cremation as a form of idolatry. "In the Talmud (Ab. Zarah, I,3) we find, among the references, the striking statement that 'every death which is accompanied by burning is looked upon as idolatry.'"[50] Orthodox and Conservative Jews continue to insist on this principle and prohibit the burial of cremains in their cemeteries. Defense of this position rests heavily on biblical precedents, ancient customs, and talmudic interpretations.

Among more liberal segments of the Jewish community, notably the Reform congregations, the practice of cremation is accepted. American Reform Rabbis are permitted to officiate at cremations in accord with a decision taken at the Central Conference of American Rabbis in 1892.[51]

The Reform position on this issue is argued from several standpoints. First, there is no biblical prohibition of the practice of cremation. Second, burial was a method of disposition that would prevent desecration and give due honor to the body. However, cremation properly conducted accomplishes the same goals. Third, biblical texts utilized by the Orthodox to promote burial and exclude cremation do not in themselves prohibit cremation and are interpreted largely by tradition.[52]

G. *Summary*

Change is taking place in American funerary tradition. Religious groups, who opposed cremation because of its pagan associations, now tolerate it within certain limits. The far-flung geographical separation of family members in a mobile society, requiring expensive transportation of bodies to the family cemetery, and the high cost of funerals and burials by inhumations have contributed to this change.

The existence of the trend, however, does not in itself justify the practice. In the next two chapters, the biblical passages relating to this issue are examined, then the arguments for and against cremation are evaluated in order to arrive at a position that is appropriate for the Christian.

4

Cremation in the Bible

The appropriateness of cremation, inhumation or any other burial practice cannot be established for the Christian on sheer social, economic, or historical grounds. This issue, like others, must be weighed against the impact of biblical teaching and example.

To peoples of the ancient Near East, the proper interment of the dead was a matter of great importance, and this was no less true of the Hebrews. When one fell into deep disfavor with another, a common Babylonian curse was, "may the earth not receive your corpse." [1]

I. BURIAL CUSTOMS

For a corpse to be ingloriously devoured by birds and animals was one of the severe curses of the Mosaic Law: "Your carcasses will be food for all the birds of the air and beasts of the earth, and there will be no one to frighten them away," (Deut. 28:26). [2] The seriousness of this judgment is all the more apparent when it is noted that even a criminal who committed a capital offense and was hanged was to be given a burial (cf. Deut. 21:22-23).

Burial among the Hebrews was regularly by means of interment with only a few exceptions[3] and consisted of three important elements: the mortuary ritual, preparation of the body, and the actual deposit of the corpse in a grave or tomb. Since the climate of Palestine was warm and since contact with a corpse produced ritual impurity, burial usually took place as soon after death as possible, usually within 24 hours (cf. Acts 5:5-6, 10). The fact that the Hebrews did not adopt cremation as an acceptable burial practice is instructive against this background. Surely a practical solution to the problems of rapid decomposition and ceremonial impurity would have been to incinerate the remains. Furthermore, since fire frequently symbolized purification, the difficulties of ritual uncleanness through contact with the corpse could be greatly reduced.

One gets the impression that there were compelling reasons why the Hebrews passed up a convenient and efficient solution to these problems in favor of simple inhumation. Such reasons become apparent when the circumstances under which human bodies were burned in Old Testament times are examined (see below).

Instructions concerning mortuary rituals and procedures are not given in great detail in Scripture, but a study of a variety of passages yields a composite picture of the general process. As soon as an individual expired, the eldest son or nearest relative present would close the eyes of the deceased if this was necessary (Gen. 46:4). Since the physical aspects of death are likened to sleep in the Bible,[4] this act was especially significant.

The mouth of the deceased was then closed and the body was washed (Acts 9:37) and anointed with aromatic ointments (John 12:7; 19:39; Mark 16:1; Luke 24:1). The body was then wrapped in cloth (normally linen, cf. Matt. 27:59; John 11:44; 19:40), although individuals of

Entrance to an Eighth Century B.C. Hebrew tomb at Tekoa. *Photo by the Author.*

high rank would frequently be clothed in fine garments
(cf. 1 Sam. 28:14). Elaborate funerary assemblages at-
tended the burial of individuals of important political or
social rank, as evidenced by both biblical[5] and archaeological data.

Embalming was not part of Hebrew burial ritual,
but the bodies of both Jacob and Joseph were mummified
since they died in Egypt where the practice was common
(Gen. 50:2, 3, 26).[6] While a coffin was used for burial of
Joseph (Gen. 50:26), this was not normally the case
among the Hebrews. During New Testament times, bones
were frequently collected after the flesh had decomposed
and placed in small stone boxes called ossuaries.

After the corpse was washed, treated with oils and
spices, and wrapped, it was carried to the tomb on a
wooden bier, usually by friends, servants, or relatives
(2 Sam. 3:31). Loud cries of sorrow were produced by
professional mourners as well as members of the family.[7]
Canaanite mourning ritual frequently included cutting
or mutilating the flesh, but this was expressly forbidden
by the law (Lev. 19:27–28; 21:5; Deut. 14:1).

The place of burial could be a simple grave, cave or
a rock-cut tomb. The latter were usually large enough to
be used by members of a family over a lengthy period of
time.

The biblical record of burial is clear that inhumation
was the only acceptable practice among both Jews and
Christians. Although the practice of burning the human
body is not absent from the Old Testament; when it
appears, it is cast in a negative light.[8]

There are no less than 15 Hebrew words used in the
Old Testament to describe the act of burning.[9] The most
common of these is the verb *sarap*, which occurs 117
times,[10] and seven of these occurrences have reference to
burning corpses or bones to ashes.[11]

A careful study of the biblical data indicates that

human corpses were subject to incineration for only one of four reasons. These are discussed below.

II. REASONS FOR INCINERATION

A. *Human Sacrifice*

Some of the most tragic passages in the Old Testament describe the utterly degraded activities of some Hebrews who had succumbed to Canaanite influences by sacrificing their children. To what extent this was practiced by the people in Israel (or elsewhere in the ancient Near East for that matter) is not clear. While mention is made of the practice among the Canaanites and some Hebrews, it is absent in Ugaritic literature.[12] There is some literary evidence that human sacrifice was practiced in Phoenicia and from there was carried to Carthage, where it became widespread.[13] Recent excavations at ancient Carthage have provided grim evidence of just how common this practice had become.[14]

Even though human sacrifice was strictly forbidden by Mosaic law (Lev. 18:21; Deut. 12:31), some Israelites,[15] including King Ahaz[16] and King Manasseh,[17] practiced it. It is also possible that the judge, Jephthah, sacrificed his daughter in fulfillment of a vow (Judges 11:30-40).[18]

Clearly, God detested the practice of burning the human body in this manner to appease false deities. Not only did the prophets protest the practice, but the sites where children were sacrificed were destroyed as part of Josiah's reforms (2 Kings 23:10). It is entirely possible, therefore, that one of the reasons the Hebrews avoided the practice of cremation is that it too closely resembled the banned practice of human sacrifice.

B. *Special Punishment*

The burning of an individual was one of four death

penalties imposed by biblical law for offenses relating to sexual promiscuity (Lev. 20:14; 21:9). In this connection it is interesting to observe Judah's demand that his daughter-in-law, Tamar, be burned to death when he learned that she had become pregnant by acting the part of a prostitute (Gen. 38:24). Of course, his perspective on the whole matter changed dramatically when it was revealed that he was the father of the child (Gen. 38:25–30)!

When Achan and his family violated the restrictions that the Lord had placed on taking booty from Jericho (Josh. 6:17–19), they were stoned to death and their bodies cremated (Josh. 7:15, 25). So despicable was their rebellion that they were not even buried in a tomb, but a large pile of rocks was piled over their ashes as a reminder of the seriousness of their crime (Josh. 7:26).[19]

In several instances, individuals were destroyed by fire as a direct judgment of God. Aaron's sons, Nadab and Abihu, were consumed by fire because of their improper sacrifices (Lev. 10:1–2). It would appear that they had only been partially burned because the sons of Uzziel, Aaron's uncle, were commanded to carry their corpses "still in their tunics" outside the camp (Lev. 10:4–5).

Fire was also employed by God to judge those who complained about their hardships in the desert (Num. 11:1–3), as well as 250 well-known community leaders who opposed the leadership of Moses and Aaron (Num. 16:1–3, 35). From these events it is easy to understand how fire became a common symbol of judgment, and, therefore, was used appropriately in the destruction of idols.[20]

Obviously, the destruction of an individual by fire in judgment hardly provided a positive incentive for the burial practice of cremation. This fact, coupled with the horrors of burning children in sacrifice, must have had a dramatic impact upon the ancient Hebrews as they contemplated alternatives in burial practice. One writer observed the following: "The teaching of the Old Testament, clearly enough, is that the burning of the human body is only right when a sin peculiar for its hideousness is awarded a penalty designed to show the hatred with which it is regarded by God."[21]

With this as background, it would have been most difficult for the Hebrew to have utilized cremation for the disposition of a corpse under any circumstances except those in which he wanted to express disdain for the deceased.

C. Desecration of the Dead

When a prophet condemned Jeroboam's altar, he indicated that it would be desecrated, in part, by the burning of human bones upon it (1 Kings 13:1–2). Later, Josiah desecrated the altar at Bethel by the same method (2 Kings 23:15–18).[22] Since the Hebrews regarded human corpses and bones as unclean (Num. 19:11–16), it would have been particularly disdainful to burn human bones on an altar and thus to make the altar itself unclean. This was not only a dramatic way for Josiah to express his contempt for the worship sites dedicated to foreign deities, but it also represented a desecration of the remains of the deceased priests who had officiated at the altars (2 Chron. 34:5).

Again, against the background of burning bones in order to desecrate a site, it would have been impossible for the Hebrews to have viewed the cremation of a corpse with anything other than negative connotations.

There are a few instances in the Old Testament, however, where cremation of a corpse is recorded without the negative connotations observed above. In an effort to solicit biblical support for the modern practice of cremation, some have appealed to these passages as evidence that the Bible does look favorably on this practice. These passages will now be examined in some detail to determine what bearing they have on this issue.

D. *Cremation of the Dead*

There are only two instances in the Old Testament where bodies appear to have been cremated under favorable or acceptable conditions. The first of these relates to the final disposition of the bodies of Saul and his sons after their tragic death in the battle at Mt. Gilboa (1 Sam. 31:1–10). The Philistines won a decisive battle in that region, and when they discovered the bodies of Saul and his sons, they decapitated them and placed them on the wall of the city in Beth Shan. Saul's armor was put on exhibit in the temple of Ashtoreth as an evidence of the greatness of the Philistine gods. Years earlier, the ark of the Covenant had undergone the same kind of treatment, but with disastrous results for the Philistines (1 Sam. 4:11; 5:1–12).

Upon learning of the deaths of Saul and his sons and the treatment of their corpses, men from Jabesh Gilead came during the night, took the bodies from the walls, burned them, and buried the bones (1 Sam. 31:11–13). One can understand the kindness and bravery of the men of Jabesh Gilead in the light of the fact that they had been the benefactors of Saul's protection earlier (1 Sam. 11:1–11).

There is little question that the remains of Saul and his sons were actually incinerated because the Hebrew text employs the verb *sarap* to describe the incident. This word is normally used in the sense of a destructive burning rather than for ordinary kindling of a fire or for metaphorical matters like burning with anger.[23]

Not all scholars agree that this term must refer to cremation, however. G. R. Driver, for example, attempted to demonstrate that the employment of *sarap* here, as well as in other passages, was used to denote an act of "anointing with resins or spices." He argued his point by associating the Hebrew *sarap* with a Samaritan word which meant "to anoint" and cognate terms from Assur that carried the meaning "to anoint with resins."[24] Pointing to the fact that it was common for Jews to anoint the body with aromatic spices (Mark 16:1; Luke 24:1), Driver insisted that the body of Saul was not cremated, but merely anointed for burial according to Hebrew custom.

Even though this interpretation has been adopted by some,[25] the evidence for it is not convincing. The evidence that the normal use of the word describes a destructive burning is just too overwhelming to permit such an exotic meaning of the term in this passage.

It is preferable to allow the word *sarap* its normal usage and to realize that conditions existed which required the cremation of the corpses. In all probability, the bodies of Saul and his sons were in an advanced state of decomposition when discovered by the men from Jabesh Gilead, and it was necessary to burn them for hygienic purposes. F. C. Cook further argues that this procedure would have prevented any future insults to the headless corpses and that the cremation was only partial, so as to preserve the bones for later burial.[26] S. Goldman suggests that "it is possible in this case that the bodies were so badly decomposed that it was considered an affront to the dead to bury them in that state."[27]

By partially cremating the remains of Saul and his sons, the men of Jabesh Gilead, therefore, avoided possible hygienic problems and made the transport of the remains easier for a final honorable burial. That the bodies were not reduced to ashes by complete cremation is evidenced by the fact that the rescuers took the "bones" of Saul and his sons, not just remaining ashes (1 Sam. 31:13). Human "bones" elsewhere in the Old Testament always has reference to the unburned skeletal materials of the body. Observe, for example, that Josiah took the "bones" of buried priests to be burned on the false altars (2 Chron. 34:5; cf. 1 Kings 13:1-2).

A second reference to the cremation of a body appears in Amos 2:1 as the basis for God's judgment upon the nation of Moab: "For three sins of Moab, even for four, I will not turn back my wrath. Because he burned, as if to lime, the bones of Edom's king" (Amos 2:1). It is generally agreed that burning of this king did not take place while he was alive, but represents the complete cremation of the corpse.[28]

The circumstances surrounding the death of this Edomite king and the reasons for the cremation of his body are not given in the text, but it is clear that it was the act of cremation which precipitated God's displeasure and later judgment. This passage had led James Fraser to argue that "if there is any verse in the Bible that positively emphasizes God's disapproval of the burning of human bodies, it is this."[29]

Significantly, God's anger was not directed against Hebrews who cremated this body, but Moabites who were not part of the covenant community of faith. Furthermore, it is apparent that there were no extenuating circumstances that surrounded the death of the king in Edom which could have motivated the Moabites to cremate the body. In the case of Saul and his sons, as in the case of those who died in the military devastation of a city (Amos 6:9-10), no condemnation of the crematory acts was forthcoming because there were special circumstances, which made incineration of the bodies a reasonable act. Amos 2:1, therefore, records an event where the cremation of the body was viewed unfavorably.

The final Old Testament passage which makes reference to cremation is Amos 6:9-10:

If ten men are left in one house, they too will die. And if a relative who is to burn the bodies comes to carry them out of the house and asks anyone still hiding there, "Is anyone with you?" and he says, "No," then he will say, "Hush!" We must not mention the name of the LORD (*NIV*).

Two specific problems are associated with the interpretation of these texts. One relates to the identity of the individual who comes to the house and the other whether he is the same person as the "burner." Most scholars appear to favor the idea that the visitor and the burner are one and the same individual.

As was the case with the interpretation of 1 Sam. 31:12, there are those who maintain that an act of cremation is not described in the above verses. Following G. R. Driver, they argue that "the reference is not, however, to the burning of the body, but the burning of spices in honor of the dead (cf. Jer. 34:5; 2 Chron. 16:14; 21:19)."[30]

Ahlstrom suggests that the kinsmen took the bones out of the house and burned them as an act of punishment and to make a standard funeral impossible,[31] a view that has not gained wide acceptance. Most commentators regard the passage as a reference to the cremation of corpses as the result of a military slaughter or a plague at the site.[32]

The death of ten men in one house represents a carnage of staggering proportions, which probably required the cremation of the remains in order to avoid plagues that would likely ravage the land where death continues to putrefy the air. This passage, like the account of Saul and his sons, represents unusual circumstances in which simple inhumation was not possible or was hygienically unwise. It should seem obvious, therefore, that such a passage cannot be employed in defense of cremation as a normal practice.

Clearly, the burning of a corpse was permitted in extenuating circumstances among the ancient Hebrews, but the practice was never accepted as a desirable or preferred burial mode. While the Old Testament provides three clear references to cremation, none alter the fact that the only accepted burial practice among the Hebrews was simple interment of the body.

III. CREMATION IN THE NEW TESTAMENT

The New Testament contains no reference to cremation unless one should mistake the language of Paul in 1 Cor. 13:3. He states that, "If I give all I possess to the poor and surrender my body to the flames, but have not love, I gain nothing" (*NIV*). There is almost universal agreement that the phrase "surrender my body to the flames" is not a reference to cremation. Actually, the statement is capable of two possible interpretations. Some

One of three arcosolia with crosses on either side in Abila Tomb J-4. The tomb was originally prepared in the 2nd century A.D., then re-used by Christians (who cut the crosses) in the 6th cent. A.D. A pillow cut in the stone indicated that the burials were by inhumation. *Photo by John J. Davis.*

suggest that Paul is referring to some form of branding connected with slavery, while most commentators see this as a reference to an extreme form of martyrdom.[33]

In accordance with well established Jewish custom, all burials recorded in the New Testament are by inhumation. The bodies of the rich man (Luke 16:22), John the Baptist (Mark 6:29), Lazarus (John 11:17–19), Ananias and Sapphira (Acts 5:6, 10), Stephen (Acts 8:2), and, most significantly, Christ (Matt. 27:57–61; 1 Cor. 15:4) were all placed in tombs following death. Since the despised Romans practiced cremation in Palestine, it would have been strange, indeed, for the Jews to have utilized it.

IV. SUPPOSED REFERENCES
TO CREMATION IN THE BIBLE

Several other texts in the Old Testament have been regarded as references to the cremation of some of Israel's kings. Regarding the death of Asa, it is recorded that "they buried him in the tomb that he had cut for himself in the City of David. They laid him on a bier covered with spices and various blended perfumes, and they made a huge fire in his honor" (2 Chron. 16:14, *NIV*). The issue in this verse is the meaning of the phrase "they made a huge fire in his honor."

When Jehoram died of an incurable disease, it is recorded that "his people made no fire in his honor, as they had for his fathers" (2 Chron. 21:19, *NIV*). Once again there is reference to fire in connection with the death of the king.

The final passage making allusion to fire at the funeral of a king is found in Jer. 34:5 where Zedekiah is promised that "they will make a fire in your honor."

The issue in all three accounts is whether the fires are references to cremation or some other act. Commentators agree that these are not references to cremation, but the burning of spices as a commemorative act for the king.[34] The clue to the function of fire in these funerary rites is found in 2 Chron. 16:14 where reference is made to the presence of "spices and various blended perfumes" with the body. Evidently, such materials were burned as part of the funerary ritual.[35]

V. CONCLUSION

Both the Old and New Testaments make it clear that among the Jews the only acceptable form of burial under normal circumstances was interment of the body. The partial cremation of Saul and his sons (1 Sam. 31:12) and the burning of numerous bodies left from the devastation of a city (Amos 6:10) were necessitated by special circumstances and clearly did not reflect the normal burial traditions of the Hebrews.

A very dark shadow is cast on the act of cremation when God soundly condemned Moab for reducing the bones of an Edomite king to ashes (Amos 2:1). It must be concluded, therefore, that while the Bible does not provide specific instruction on funeral rituals or procedures, the weight of historic evidence is that the preferred method of burial was by inhumation.

5

A Christian Perspective

Developing a biblically supported Christian perspective on the subject of cremation is both delicate and difficult. It is delicate because discussions of funerary traditions have generally been hidden under a cloak of sanctity, and now that they have surfaced with the rise of cremation, much of the response has been emotional rather than rational.

It is difficult because the Bible does not address the issue directly, and thus one is forced to examine traditional practices, theological symbolism, and contextual nuances for an answer. If one is honest with the evidence at hand, the conclusion must be one of what is more spiritually appropriate or advisable rather than which method is inherently right or wrong.

The purpose of this chapter is to examine the arguments for the practices of cremation as well as inhumation. Against the background of biblical truth, theological symbolism and practical wisdom, some guidelines for the Christian to follow in making decisions in this most complex area are suggested.

I. THE CASE FOR CREMATION

Unless Amos 2:1 is regarded as a direct and conscious prohibition of cremation, there are no passages in Scripture that directly address the issue in the form of a command. This is not to conclude that there is a total absence of data that might bear on the subject. It simply acknowledges that a number of factors must be considered before decisions can be reached regarding appropriate burial practices. The following discussion represents the principal arguments offered by those who promote the practice of cremation.

A. *Fire Can Symbolize Good*

This argument is perhaps one of the weakest in that the preponderance of biblical material points to rather negative perceptions about fire and incineration of the human body.

William Phipps argues as follows:

> The Israelites generally buried their dead, but the bodies of their first royalty, Saul and his sons, were honored by cremation after death in battle. In biblical times fire was often regarded as symbolic of the divine presence, so it was appropriate to feature fire in sacred ceremonies. God was represented by a flaming torch in an encounter with Abraham, and at Mt. Sinai "the appearance of the glory of the Lord was like a devouring fire" (Exod. 24:17). . . .
>
> . . . The early Christians affirmed that "God is a consuming fire" (Heb. 12:29), but despite the hallowed association they gave to fire, and the absence of a biblical prohibition against cremation, the traditional Jewish burial custom was adopted.[1]

While it is quite true God is referred to as a "consuming fire," it is in a warning context (see Heb. 12:25–26) designed to underscore the awesome destructive power of God in judgment. In fact, as was demonstrated in Chapter 4 of this book, the incineration of the human body in Old Testament contexts is nearly always in a negative context. Child sacrifice and the burning of judged criminals are just two examples of this phenomenon.

It is also doubtful that one should refer to the incineration of Saul and his sons by the men of Jabesh-gilead as an act by which they were "honored by cremation." The biblical text states in matter-of-fact fashion that they were merely "burned." To introduce the word "honor" is to assume the conclusion for which one is arguing.

Indeed, one must ask why, if the ancient Hebrews and early Christians regarded fire as "hallowed," they so consistently avoided the practice of cremation? In all likelihood, the broader biblical usage of the term, coupled with widespread pagan ideas associated with it, made it difficult to associate cremation with anything "good," such as honoring the dead.

B. *It Is More Economical*

There is no question about the value of this argument. The average American is spending about $3500 on embalming, casket, vault, funeral service, and interment in a privately purchased plot.[2] Some cemeteries do not require a vault and this would reduce the overall price by about $370. Many funeral packages are much higher than this, however, as additional services and goods are sold by the funeral home. If the body of the deceased must be flown from overseas, it could cost an additional $2000 to $3500, depending on the distance and the country.

The cost of a cremation, on the other hand, is in the range of $600 to $800 on the average, although it must be acknowledged that this amount can be reduced or increased depending on location, elaborateness of materials, etc. The actual cost of cremation in Indiana usually costs between $120 and $175. To this, of course, must be added the cost of a coffin to transport the body to the crematory, an urn, and any additional funeral home services.

The high degree of American family mobility has complicated the practice of inhumation considerably. Many families own plots near their original residences, and there is frequently a desire to be buried with other family members in that plot. Transporting the body over long distances is a significant expense, which is easily avoided when the body is cremated and the remains shipped or carried.

Of course, families will need to decide on the merits of the alternatives. If inhumation is deeply desired, then perhaps burial where the death occurred whether in a foreign land or another part of this country, should be considered. On the other hand, some have felt that the cost of transporting the body was worth memorializing the individual by burial in his or her homeland.

Some Christians have felt that the expense of flying the body of a loved one home from a foreign country is not appropriate in the light of other values. They have opted for cremation followed by burial and a memorial service in this land with the money saved going to a church, mission organization, or Christian college with whom the deceased had special association. It is not uncommon for missionaries or those working overseas to provide living wills that specify this type of burial and memorialization or request that burial occur in the land in which they die. Such a living will can be of great assistance to family members at the time of death by alleviating feelings of guilt that may accompany choosing certain burial options.

C. *It Saves Space*

In countries like Japan and Singapore, space is very

limited and cremation is often practiced out of practical necessity. In a few metropolitan areas of the United States space for cemeteries has also become a critical problem. In these situations there is no doubt about the benefits of cremation as opposed to inhumation.

However, this argument does not have universal application because most countries still have adequate space for interments. More than 1000 individuals can be buried in one acre of land.[3] If bodies are stacked or reburied as is done in parts of Europe, many more could be buried per acre.

The scarcity of land in large metropolitan areas has put great pressure on the preservation of existing cemeteries. Many cities have been forced to relocate thousands of burials in order to utilize the land for critically needed services. In 1946, for example, more than 47,000 burials were removed from Lafayette Cemetery in South Philadelphia and reburied in another area to allow for development of the property as a playground area.[4]

D. *It Is Ecologically More Desirable*

There are actually two lines of reasoning involved in this argument. The first relates to the burial apparatus. Metals and hardware, which are very much a part of expensive inhumations, are used for a brief viewing ceremony. The nonbiodegradable materials are placed in the ground, where they serve no useful function. In contrast, "when a sturdy woodpulp container, costing a few dollars, is used for cremation, no nails, hinges or other metal pieces are left mixed in with the ashes. The few pounds of remains, pulverized to a sand-like consistency, can then be distributed in a garden or forest as a token aid to the growth of new life."[5]

Second, there is the issue of hygienic integrity of the burial area. In much of Japan, inhumation is considered "unsanitary, for rocky soil permits only shallow graves. These are soon water soaked by heavy rains and exposed to air and animals."[6]

It is argued that some graveyards have been the source of disease and epidemics.[7] The apparent hygienic benefits of cremation have been underscored in the recent history of England.

> The subject of employing cremation for the bodies of those who die of contagious disease is important. Such diseases include small pox, scarlet fever, diphtheria, tuberculosis, enteric relapsing and puerperal fevers, the number of deaths from which in the United Kingdom in 1926 was upwards of 94,000. In cremation complete disinfection takes place by means of the high temperature to which the body is exposed.[8]

While the thrust of the basic argument above is certainly valid, it should be noted that it is not clear, nor scientifically established, that all 94,000 deaths were directly attributable to inhumation, as is implied in the statement.

The full and scientific validity of this argument, furthermore, depends on a number of factors such as the type of soil, grading in the area, and the containers employed.

E. *It is Therapeutic for the Survivors*

Grief therapy has long been a consideration in funeral ritual and burial, and the issue continues to occupy a prominent place in debate over cremation. It has been assumed that preservation of the body for viewing is the best form of therapy for the grieving survivors and allows for the easiest transition to the new circumstances of life.

But such a notion is not universally held in the Christian community. Phipps states the issue as follows:

> Finding no value in slow decomposition, some see no point in

having morticians temporarily arrest this inevitable process by replacing the blood with embalming fluid. Nor do they find comfort in being deceived by cosmetics into thinking the body is "just sleeping." On the contrary, a clean incineration which quickly reduces the body of the deceased to its component elements can be therapeutic for mourners by expressing the final severance of the physical bond.[9]

Richard L. Morgan writes in a similar vein:

Cremation can be therapeutic for the grieving family by finalizing the loss, hallowing memories of the person, and affirming hope for a glorified body.[10]

It is further asserted that "traditional funeral customs do far more to block grief by their denial of death and their morbid preoccupation with the body of the deceased."[11]

While it may be true that an excessively long preoccupation with the corpse might be a detriment to the grief process, some thanatologists are concerned about those who cremate the deceased without any viewing at all. Immediate cremation and the exclusion of any funeral service may well be a form of grief denial which could lead to emotional problems later. Alan Wolfelt argues that, "when emotions are repressed or denied, they often find detours that may be a threat to both physical and emotional health. If bereaved people are given the opportunity for genuine expression of feelings of grief, they are more able to work toward successful reconciliation of the mourning process."[12]

Wolfelt further observes that, "seeing the body challenges the natural wish to avoid the reality of death. While, at the same time, encouraging healthy acceptance of the death."[13]

Determining the nature and process of successful grief therapy is a difficult one, indeed. Much of the therapeutic value of any funerary ritual depends on cultural conditioning, prior understanding of the death experience, the circumstances of the death itself, the relationship to the deceased, and the emotional make-up of the survivors. While one person will find cremation to be "barbaric, nightmarish," another views it as "simple, fitting and decent."[14]

F. *It Prevents Certain Abuses*

Proponents of inhumation often argue that interment provides a final resting place that is most fitting for a perpetual and honorable memorial. Cremationists, however, argue that this notion is not in accord with the facts of today's modern world, where many cemeteries are being destroyed through vandalism or development. Everett MacNair writes, "in many cases it is unfair for cemetery companies to promise perpetual care. Many cemeteries have been abandoned in order to provide room for expansion. Five cemeteries in San Francisco have had to be abandoned to make room for industry and residential areas."[15]

The controversial exhumation of more than 47,000 burials from the south Philadelphia Lafayette Cemetery and redeposit in unmarked graves is a case in point. Instead of reburial in marked sites as had been agreed upon, many of the remains were dumped into large unmarked trenches.[16]

Of course, it might also be argued that cremation does not offer anything better for the remains if they are placed in a cemetery setting. Natural disasters, development projects, and vandalism put all marked burials at risk in today's world.

G. *Inhumation is a Desecration of the Body*

This argument for cremation will startle many because proponents of inhumation have argued that *crema-*

tion is a desecration of the body. This has been true especially among the clergy, many of whom maintain that cremation of the body desecrates God's creation. Mary Comyns sees it differently, however,

> For centuries we have buried our dead, believing that by so doing we have cared for them with utmost tenderness; but what is the result of that so-called tenderness? Simply this: we deliberately consign them to a slow process of decomposition, which, if we could watch its varying stages, would fill our minds with horror. It is in reality a desecration of the body, happily within our power to prevent, and our earnest thought today, must be given to the consideration of this question which has on the one side mistaken sentiment, on the other sanitation.[17]

However, this argument appears a bit strained against the weight of historical evidence, which includes incineration for the purposes of sacrificing children, murdering Christian martyrs, and punishing criminals (as in the case of Achan and his family [Josh. 7]).

H. *Not All Individuals Cremated are Pagans*

Those who criticize the practice of cremation frequently assert that most of those who desire to be cremated are enemies of the church, unbelievers of the worst sort, or humanists. James Fraser writes, for example, that "the disposal of the body by cremation has in recent years been largely the choice of unbelievers and notorious characters. It is true that some good-living people have requested it, but you will agree that the vast majority have been questionable characters."[18]

While it is certainly true that some of Europe's worst criminals and America's enemies of the church have been cremated, it seems to be a bit reckless to generalize in the fashion done above. It does not necessarily follow that because some individuals choose cremation to make a certain religious or social statement, that all who choose it are making the same statement. It must be remembered that the Egyptians faithfully practiced inhumation, but their notions about the future life and the nature of death were clearly not biblical. Are all who practice inhumation perpetrating Egyptian concepts of the afterlife?

Clearly, not all who have been cremated were enemies of the church. This is plainly illustrated by the fact that all bodies interred in Westminster Abbey have been cremated, including those of the last two Archbishops of Canterbury.[19]

Noted Bible teacher and expositor G. Campbell Morgan favored cremation. "As to cremation there is certainly nothing in Scripture to forbid it. We need to remember that cremation is the hastening of the process that would take time through burial. Personally, I am in favor of cremation, and it does not invalidate any biblical view of personality."[20]

The grandson of G. Campbell Morgan follows this view when he writes, "cremation witnesses to this faith, for our hope does not lie in what undertakers do to our bodies at death, but in the power of God who raised Jesus from the dead."[21]

I. *Summary*

When all arguments for cremation are considered, several observations can be made. First, there is no positive biblical support for the practice either by example or direct command. Whatever conclusions may be drawn in favor of cremation from a biblical perspective must be largely arguments from silence. The common mode of burial in both the Old and New Testaments was inhumation.

Second, cremation defense based on arguments from spacial considerations, sanitary concerns, and economy does have validity given certain circumstances.

Third, there is evidence that many who select cremation do so out of either philosophical interests or life style commitments. Thomas E. Spencer has documented a number of desires motivating the practice of cremation including the desire to shock, to show toughness and bravery, to be self-effacing, to preserve one's identity, to satisfy romantic impulses or aesthetic sensitivities and the desire to be regarded as an enlightened person.[22] It is also apparent that, in some cases, cremation is selected in order to deny the grief and mourning process.

II. THE CASE FOR INHUMATION

The case for inhumation is strong as evidenced by its universal popularity and great antiquity. The predominance of inhumation in the Christian community is an indication that this mode of burial has best met the biblical and theological concerns of the church. The most important arguments for inhumation are as follows.

A. *Inhumation was the normal practice of the Hebrews*

The principal means of the disposition of the body in the Old Testament was by simple inhumation. In fact, the Hebrews often went to great lengths to accomplish this end. Note the efforts of Abraham to purchase a burial cave for Sarah in Gen. 23:1-20 and Joseph's instructions regarding the body of Jacob and his own (Gen. 50:1-14, 25-26 cf. Ex. 13:19 and Josh. 24:32).

B. *When God had to care for the body of Moses, he chose burial.*

A question worth raising is "what would God do if He were responsible for the disposition of a corpse?" The answer to this question is found in Deut. 34:5-6. "So Moses the servant of the LORD died there in the land of Moab, according to the word of the LORD. And He buried him in the valley in the land of Moab, opposite Beth-peor; but no man knows his burial place unto this day" (NASB,

Underlining added). This act of God provides the believer with important evidence that burial of the body is preferred to any other method of disposition.

C. *Inhumation Follows the Example of Christ and the Early Church*

For Christians both past and present this has been a most compelling influence. Jesus' burial by inhumation (Matt. 27:57-61) and his later resurrection (John 20:1-30) provide the model for the believer's hope. In fact, Jesus was very specific about the issue when He stated, "Destroy this temple (His body) and I will raise it up" (John 2:19).

Jesus seems to have chosen this method of burial when He acknowledged Mary's anointing of His head (Mark 14:3-9) and feet (John 12:3-8) as preparation for His burial.

Frequently, cremation has been used as a personal statement of belief that death ends all. Again, it must be noted that Jesus and His Jewish contemporaries knew of the practice of cremation, but chose not to adopt it because of what it represented among the Romans.

Saints in Jerusalem like Ananias, Sapphira and Stephen were not cremated, but buried.[23] The Christians at Rome took the bodies of St. Justin and his companions and "buried them in a fitting place."[24] The burials of St. Epipodius and St. Alexander at Lyons were on the same order.[25]

Furthermore, the early church did not assume that the resurrection depended on the preservation of the body as some of the Roman officials had concluded. It was clearly understood that whatever happened to this physical body would in no way affect the final resurrection. St. Ignatius the Martyr was quite unconcerned about the manner in which his body was disposed and wrote so to the Romans.

> Suffer me to be eaten by the beasts, through whom I may attain to God. I am God's wheat, and I am ground by the teeth of wild beasts that I may be found pure bread of Christ. Rather entice the wild beasts that they may become my tomb and leave no trace of my body that when I fall asleep I be not burdensome to any. Then shall I truly be a disciple of Jesus Christ when the world shall not even see my body.[26]

Tatian, speaking of the resurrection expresses similar sentiments.

> And though dispersed through rivers and seas or torn in pieces by wild beasts, I am laid up in the storehouse of a wealthy Lord ... Yet God the sovereign when He so wishes will restore the substance that is visible to Him alone to its former state.[27]

In spite of these clear testimonies of hope, and "out of the hatred for this Christian belief, they did all in their power to prevent the bodies of the martyrs from being buried. Various tortures were devised by which their bodies would be completely destroyed."[28]

D. *Inhumation Acknowledges The Sanctity of the Body*

Christians regard the human body as the product of special creation (Gen. 1:26-27; 2:7), and when an individual receives Christ as Lord and Savior, his or her body becomes a "temple of the Holy Spirit" (1 Cor. 6:19-20). In life, therefore, the body has special value as the object of God's redemptive activity, and it is deemed inappropriate to destroy it with fire. Since man's body originated from the dust (Gen. 2:7; 3:19), there has been a desire to return it to the dust or earth in the best form possible as an act of reverence to God who created it.

John Jamieson reflects the sentiments of the early Christians as follows:

> By the primitive Christians it was objected to cremation, that the practice involved in it the idea of inhumanity to the body. Hence Tertullian having remarked, that some of the Gentiles disapproved of the mode of burning because they wished to spare the soul, which hovered over the body after death, subjoins, "But we have another reason, that of piety, not as flattering the reliques of the soul, but as detesting cruelty even to the body; because, being itself, man does not deserve to be subjected to a penal death."[29]

Christians have always concluded that whether dead or alive, the body belongs to God because of redemption and sanctification (cf. Rom. 8:23; Heb. 10:10). On this matter

Origin wrote, "It is the reasonable soul which we honor, and we commit its bodily organs with honors to the grave."[30]

E. *Inhumation Better Symbolizes the Hope of the Resurrection*

The apostle Paul refers to the placement of the body in the earth as "sowing" (1 Cor. 15:42-44; cf. v. 37), thus using an agricultural metaphor.

Even though it is planted as a whole but dead "seed," it will ultimately be raised. Christians have long felt that sowing a "natural body" (v. 44) is best symbolized by inhumation.

Further, the image of the dead "sleeping" (v. 51; cf. 1 Thess. 4:13-18) is best preserved by interment of the body rather than the cremains of that body.

Finally, the biblical doctrine of the final judgment of the wicked by fire (Rev. 20:14; cf. John 15:6) makes cremation inappropriate for the one has been saved from such a judgment.

As the careful reader will have noted by now, much of the Christian attitude toward burial has been influenced by the examples of burial in Scripture and a desire to most accurately symbolize the belief in the resurrection. For one who is not a Christian and, therefore, not sensitive to these factors, the only issues that really have influence on burial method are family tradition, economy, space, or emotion. For this reason cremation has been more readily accepted by the secular community than by those with theological sensitivities.

F. *Cremation Can Be an Aid to Crime*

If a victim of a crime is cremated, then there is no possibility of later examining the remains for the purpose of acquiring evidence. "It has been stated by those who are in a position to know, that, in the detection of criminal poisoning, a proper analysis cannot be obtained after cremation."[31]

An example of how criminals can utilize cremation was dramatically illustrated in a recent insurance-fraud scam by which a man collected $1 million on the presumed death of his partner. It was assumed that Melvin Hanson, the founder of a chain of sports clothing stores in Ohio, had died of a heart attack and his partner, John Hawkins, had his body immediately cremated. Police, however, later discovered that the body that had been cremated was not that of Hanson.

Investigators have established that it was the body of a drifter had been cremated and that Hanson is still alive. He and his partner have apparently been living lavishly off the insurance money in Florida.

In this case, thumb prints of the dead man who had been cremated were compared with the thumb prints of Hanson and it was determined that the two were not the same. Had Hanson not been required to have thumb prints taken for his driver's license, the insurance fraud might have been the perfect crime.[32]

Of more concern to law enforcement officers, however, is that fact that a person could be cremated who later is suspected as having been the victim of a crime. Cremation eliminates the possibility of forensic study of the remains. Of course, these kinds of problems could easily be avoided if the law prohibited the cremation of a suspected victim of crime until a forensic examination of the body could be made.

Most states require that there be a 48-hour waiting period before cremation occurs. There is such a 48-hour waiting period in Indiana and before cremation is performed, there must be a signed death certificate filed with the local board of health, which issues the burial permit. There must also be consent of an "authorizing agent"—the surviving spouse, adult child or other person legally entitled to order the cremation. If there is no spouse, all the adult children must agree before there can be a cremation.

G. *Cremains Are Sometimes Scandalously Handled*

This argument against cremation is not a compelling one because the same can be said of inhumation. Grave robbery for jewels is both an ancient and modern practice. Cemeteries can be destroyed and memorial stones stolen, removed or destroyed.

But it must be admitted that abuses of the ash remains of cremation are more common than abuse of the remains of inhumation. The ease with which cremains can be transported has led to a number of abuses in their handling and final deposit. In California, for example, it was assumed by thousands of people that the ash remains committed to the Neptune Society would be scattered from an airplane over the Pacific Ocean or over the trees high in the Sierra Nevada. Investigations in 1984 revealed that the remains of more than 9000 people had been taken by car to a ten acre site in rural Volcano in the Sierra foothills and dumped.

The event was illegal on two grounds. First, it is against California law to co-mingle human remains, and second, it represented a violation of contract.[33]

Cremains of individuals have been left stacked in mortuaries or have been mixed with other cremains. Vessels have broken while en route through the mail and the ashes lost. And there have been family squabbles over who should have possession of the ashes.

A recent letter to "Dear Abby" exemplifies the last issue. A man died having been married to a second wife for only a year and a half. He was cremated and his widow kept the cremains in her bedroom. His daughter objected to this and wanted the cremains buried in the family plot. She argued that since she had been with her father for 23 years as compared to only a year and a half for the second wife, she should have possession of the cremains.[34]

California residents were shocked when a Jan. 20, 1987, discovery revealed that a nondescript building in the desert was not producing pottery as had been advertised, but was illegally cremating dozens of human bodies in a furnace at one time.

Will Wentworth became suspicious of the operation when he recognized the smell of the black smoke as that of burning bodies. He drove out to Oscar Ceramics and opened one of the massive brick furnaces and a burning foot fell out. Scattered around the shop were trash cans filled with human remains.

Later investigations revealed that the owner of the crematory-The Lamb Funeral Home in Pasadena-had been selling body parts. "Eyes, brains and gold-filled teeth were sold without knowledge of relatives, while workers competed to see who could stuff the most bodies into the ancient crematory ovens, according to witnesses."[35]

These grisly discoveries illustrate the temptation that exists for the unscrupulous mortician who is out to made a fast buck on a rapidly growing industry.

While the above is not by any means a conclusive argument against cremation, it does point out that serious problems do exist in the cremation industry and careful regulation is needed to prevent abuses of the cremains.

III. CONCLUSION

In the light of all foregoing discussions in this volume, this writer concludes that it is preferable for the Christian to bury by inhumation whenever possible.

The words of this conclusion have been carefully chosen. They do not state that it is sinful or evil to practice cremation because the biblical, theological, and historical evidence does not support such strong language. This conclusion recognizes that much of the argument for inhumation does not come from direct Scriptural command, but from analogy, example, and symbolism. Even though these components are not inconsequential, they form a basis for preference rather than dogma.

This conclusion also recognizes the legitimacy of cremation under certain limited circumstances. For example, cremation may be required by state law (as in parts of Japan). Also, cremation may be the only practical means of burial because of a disaster or an outbreak of a deadly disease. Cremation may be desirable in order to economically transport home an individual who has died in a foreign land. Further, cremation may be preferred when local environmental conditions make inhumation unfeasible. Additionally, there is nothing *inherently* evil with the cremation of the body.

The body will ultimately be reduced to bone remains in inhumation, as is the case in cremation. The difference in reaching that point is time and method. Some feel that having a viewing and funeral service before cremation gives due respect to the body and by cremating the remains, the overall burial cost is significantly reduced.

Nevertheless, while there may be nothing inherently evil with the act of cremation, it should be remembered that the history of the practice and its associations have been largely negative and out of harmony with the Bible's high view of the body.

The questions the thoughtful Christian must ask are, "How even in burial can I best reflect biblical values and teaching? In the disposition of my body how can I best exhibit my Christian values and a hope for the resurrection?"

A question frequently asked is, "Should a pastor officiate at the funeral or memorial service when a Christian has been cremated?" Some would respond with an emphatic "no,"[36] but it is this writer's judgment that ministry to the living must take preference over one's personal convictions on this issue. Instructions for the Catholic clergy are helpful on this point. If the individual chose cremation as an act of defiance of church doctrine, then the priest is not to officiate. The Vatican instructions read as follows:

> The Christian funeral service is to be given to those who have chosen the cremation of their own body, unless it is certain that in making such a choice they were motivated by reasons hostile to the Christian life in accordance with what has been laid down in the Instruction of the Holy Office dated 8 May 1963, *de cadaverum crematione*, nos. 2-3.[37]

Every pastor must deal with the issue of death including burial, as a regular part of his ministry. The great tragedy of our day is that this topic is rarely part of the pulpit ministry, and too much is left to family members, friends or funeral directors. The greatest grief therapy in the world is a confident understanding of the nature of death, the victory Christ wrought over it in His resurrection, and the sure hope of the bodily resurrection of the believer.

6

Some Needed Reforms

Burial of the dead has become a costly affair in American society, and in recent years many of those costs have come under careful scrutiny by a variety of writers. While most funeral directors have been sensitive and responsible in giving attention to burial needs, there have been a disturbing number of instances in which bereaving people have been exploited.

A number of writers have taken a close look at American funerary practices and the costs associated with them and have called for a reevaluation of many of these practices. Among the more notable books have been Jessica Mitford's *The American Way of Death*[1] and Ruth Harmer's *The High Cost of Dying*.[2] Two of the most balanced treatments of the funeral and its appropriate values are the works of Paul E. Irion entitled, *The Funeral: Vestige or Value?*[3] and Alan D. Wolfelt's, *Death and Grief: A Guide for Clergy.*[4]

Of course, the funeral industry cannot take all the blame for the problems that have developed, for in most cases they have merely moved into vacuums created by an uninterested clergy and an uninformed public. The end result has been very costly funerals with activities and materials that are only marginally significant to the burial process. Once certain funerary traditions are established, they seem to take on such sanctimonious qualities that no one dares to question their validity. But this, I should hasten to add, is not a new problem.

> The Church established special burial grounds to discourage pagan practices connected with burials such as placing elaborate collections of funerary objects. These were only marginally successful, however. . . .
>
> . . . These seventh century burial grounds often display signs of superstitious precautions in greater variety and concentration than in earlier cemeteries belonging to a totally heathen era.[5]

By the end of the seventh century, however, the Church was able to break many of these pagan traditions and have bodies interred in a church yard with proper Christian rites.[6]

The modern funeral in this country is a reflection of the inability of the American to face the reality of death, and as a result, it has become more and more a "conspiracy of evasion."[7] As these questionable trends have developed, Christians have been strangely silent. There has been a subtle process of cultural and economic accommodation that probably would have not taken place in any other area of human experience.

It is to these concerns that attention is now turned in an attempt to strengthen the Christian testimony in the modern funeral process.

I. DISPLAY OF THE BODY

One of the greatest concerns in modern funeral practice is the inordinate amount of attention given to the display of the body. On this issue, Ernest Morgan observes that, "to many religious people of all faiths, and secular-minded as well, the preoccupation of a funeral with the dead body represents a misplacing of emphasis, no matter how thoughtful the sermon, how impressive the surroundings or how gracious the funeral director."[8]

Richard Morgan remarks, "It is pagan to make the body of the deceased an object on display for spectators. It is pagan to 'view the remains' to see if they 'look natural,' especially when morticians remove all evidence of death to soften its horror."[9]

It is too strong to call any viewing of the body "pagan," but the amount of money spent on this aspect of the funeral is, at times, scandalous. Cosmetologists, colored lighting, a slumber room, innerspring mattresses for the coffin, and expensive satin or silk coffin liners are just a few items that have escalated the costs of the average funeral. Instead of the body being prepared for burial, it is prepared for display.

Embalming is not required by state law except in cases when public health might be endangered and some instances when transportation is to be made by common carrier to another place. Embalming was not practiced in the United States until the Civil War, when it was started so that the bodies of soldiers could be shipped home for burial. In the modern world the desire for long viewing periods has required this practice.

The usual explanation for this ritual is that it is proper to "show love and respect for the departed." But it might be argued from a biblical point of view that this is a rather strange notion. The "person" is not present at such occasions but is at home with his Lord (2 Cor. 5:8). There is, therefore, no way the deceased could appreciate the effort extended! If individuals really cared for the deceased, they would have visited and honored him or her while he or she was alive. My grandmother used to say with some emphasis, "Don't buy flowers and visit me when I'm dead, do it when I'm alive so I can enjoy it." That admonishment expresses a great deal of practical wisdom. One suspects that long viewing periods may be mere accommodations to the guilty consciences of family members who have ignored or mistreated the deceased when he or she was alive.

The display of the body at a Christian funeral service is also another concern. Funeral directors often insist that the body be displayed in an open casket at the funeral service, and the casket is usually placed in front of the audience and next to the pulpit. Nothing could be more detracting to the meaning and purpose of the service. Family members inevitably focus their attention on the body, and this produces continual weeping which clearly detracts from the message of the pastor. Instead of attention being placed on the hope of the resurrection and Christ's victory over death, the lifeless body of the deceased is on center stage.

It would be far better for the casket to be closed for the actual funeral service and located at the back of the auditorium so that full attention could be placed on the message of Scripture and the hope it brings. Furthermore, such a procedure is a good transitional step in assisting the family to understand the separation which has occurred.

One writer has suggested that a viewing period (without embalming where possible) be limited to less than 24 hours with a private family funeral following.[10] Burial within 24 hours is a tradition practiced in many countries. A memorial service could be arranged for a larger audience a day or two later.

But, again, it should be emphasized that some viewing of the body is a critical component in the grief process for most people. "As strange as it may seem, the bereaved person's mind requires evidence that the person is no longer living. The opportunity to view the body provides this evidence."[11]

For those who might be concerned about the image of the deceased lingering in the mourner's mind and hindering long term re-adjustment, Wolfelt writes that, "experience suggests that the dead image will not be the forever lasting image in the mind of the survivor. While it is the image of the person being dead that allows for the verification of the death, that very image usually fades and the living memories become everlasting."[12]

Much of the high cost of modern funerals is due to exorbitant prices for caskets and vaults. Selecting inexpensive hardware for a funeral need not rob the event of the dignity or thoughtfulness it requires. With the average funeral costing in excess of $4,500 (not including a plot or vault), and many others exceeding that amount by thousands of dollars, it is time for Christians to re-evaluate this expenditure.

Some cemeteries require the use of a vault, while others do not. If a vault does not need to be used for burial, a saving of more than $400 can be realized. Of course, if cremation is chosen and there is no embalming or viewing, the total cost of the burial could be less than $500 depending on the price of the casket utilized to transport the body to the crematorium.

Whatever the choice of the Christian, less emphasis needs to be placed on the body and its surroundings and more on the hope of the Christian faith. This spiritual emphasis is one of the most important components of grief therapy for the bereaved Christian family and the greatest testimony to those who are not believers.

II THE SIZE OF THE FUNERAL SERVICE

It has become fashionable even among Christians to have large, elaborate funeral services. Such a practice is highly questionable on two grounds. First, in the light of Christian values, is this the best use of the money? Second, is this not a surrender to secular and social pressures that are not in harmony with Christianity?

Frequently believers are pressured into having large, expensive funerals because they are told by funeral directors or friends that to do otherwise is to dishonor the memory of the deceased. "After all," it is argued, "should one not be buried in a manner which reflects the social and financial standing he had in life?" But is this intention to impress people really in accord with the best values of the Christian faith? Should not the funeral be an opportunity to minister to people rather than to impress them? Paul's admonition in 1 Cor. 10:31 is just as appropriate at death as it is in life, "Whether therefore ye eat, or drink, or whatsoever ye do, do all to the glory of God."

Smith contends that "Today we have allowed funerals to become status symbols. Money is wasted because we are afraid of what others might think if the funeral is not expensive, flowers extensive, and the grave located in the 'good' section of the cemetery."[13]

Finally, it is also questionable whether large, public funeral services are in the best interest of the grieving family.

> The homegoing of a loved one is keenly felt by the immediate family. Theirs alone are feelings no one else, no matter how close a friendship may be, can fully share. Pangs of grief are felt that can be expressed only within the solitude of the family. At such a time, maximum exposure to the public hardly strengthens sorely shaken emotions: even well-intended condolences by others may further fray the already jagged nerves of the bereaved. At such a time a large, public funeral service might place loved ones on display when they may be least prepared for it.[14]

A Christian memorial service after a private family funeral might be more appropriate and effective in light of the grief experiences of the survivors, on one hand, and the desire of the family to provide a victorious witness, on the other. This would enable the family to keep the funeral costs to a minimum and still eloquently express the faith of the deceased and the family.

III. LOCATION OF THE FUNERAL SERVICE

While those not having church affiliations need to depend on the services and facilities of the funeral home, church members should utilize the church as a more appropriate setting for the funeral or memorial service. "The impersonal funeral chapels with their canned music, somber colors and isolated family rooms leave much to be desired," writes Morgan.[15]

Memorial or funeral services in the church allow for a more obvious testimony regarding the hope of the resurrection. Furthermore, from the standpoint of effective grief therapy, the presence of fellow believers in a familiar setting provides considerable spiritual and emotional reinforcement during this difficult time. "There they may praise the God of the Resurrection. And when there is no corpse present, those who come may affirm that God *is* good, rather than wonder if the person in that polished box *looks* good."[16] In addition to a more suitable setting, such a provision can keep the cost down.

IV. MINISTRY OF COMFORT

Most churches do little to prepare their members for the most emotional and traumatic event of the death of a loved one. Most pastors are well equipped to provide counsel to the widow or widower regarding funeral arrangements. Some, however, are not able to offer this service either because of time constraints or inability to remain current on funeral trends, prices, etc.

When is the last time you heard a sermon on the

Christian funeral and what it should represent? Sure, there are many eloquent messages on the nature of death and the afterlife, but little, if anything, is ever said about funeral customs, the nature and function of grief, and the values of appropriate mourning. As a result, the average church member is poorly equipped to deal with his or her personal grief and the multitude of details which arise at this very difficult time.

It would be helpful if every church had a bereavement committee made up of knowledgeable and spiritually mature businessmen and women. Such a committee could assist the pastor and family with funeral arrangements, if they had not already been cared for prior to the death. They could also provide comfort, assistance and encouragement long after other family members have left the area.

Christian businessmen on the committee could keep themselves current on regional funeral home and cemetery policies, as well as costs, and thus provide a valuable, objective assessment of alternative funeral arrangements. This would make funeral homes more accountable and prevent exploitation of individuals who are emotionally vulnerable at the time of a loved one's death.

V. THE PREPARATION OF CHILDREN AND ADOLESCENTS

Another area of serious concern has been the neglect of preparing children and adolescents for the eventuality of the death experience. Two very basic issues require consideration here: (1) Should children or adolescents attend funeral services? and (2) If so, in what manner should they be prepared for these events?

The problem of children and funerals has a long and sad history. Generally speaking, children are poorly prepared for the death and funeral of a loved one.

What prepares the adolescent in our society for an embalmed, cosmeticized body, a subdued, awkward crowd of adults who have difficulty speaking to other mourners, the often somber surroundings of the funeral parlor or church, and the smell of flowers and candle wax that will evoke memories for a lifetime? How does a teenager learn what to do *at the same time* that he or she is gripped by powerful emotions that threaten self-control?[17]

Tragically, a very negative first funeral experience for a child or adolescent can create emotional problems during that period of life and can lead to difficulties in dealing with all future funerals. Even more traumatic for a youngster is the death of another child. Is it advisable for a child to attend the funeral of another child?

Most writers agree that it is appropriate for children to attend funerals because children's fantasies regarding the event are usually worse than reality, and the funeral ritual offers a sense of closure for them just as it does for adults.[18] However, there is some concern about attendance at funerals that involve another child.

An important study of 12 children between the ages of 3–15 by J. Schowalter indicates that some emotional or behavioral problems can develop during or following a funeral. It was further concluded that children under ages six or seven years do not benefit from funeral attendance.[19]

Based on these and other studies, it has been concluded that children should not be coerced to attend a funeral, but should be allowed a choice and the decision of the child should be respected. The most noticeable behavioral problems as the result of funeral attendance appeared to be among very young children and girls.[20]

All agree that children need instruction about death and burial well before they attend a funeral service. This is best done in the Christian home during family devotions when the issue of physical death can be treated apart from the emotions of a funeral service and against the background of theological truth. All questions regarding this need not be answered on one occasion, but at appropriate times the subject of death should be reviewed. Special news events also provide an ideal time to discuss this as a family. Discussions ought to include what is expected of the child at a funeral.

An adult should remain with a child during funeral proceedings in order to provide explanations and to help when needed. Cremation provides some special challenges in explanation because some children regard this as an act which will prohibit the individual's return.[21]

VI. CONCLUSION

On the basis of historical, biblical, and experiential studies it has been concluded that the preferable method of burial practice for the Christian community is inhumation whenever possible. Cremation, however, may be preferred under special circumstances, such as when it is required by provincial law, when it is the only practical means of burial because of plague or war (cf. 1 Sam. 31:12-13; Amos 6:9-12), when it is desired to transport home an individual who has died in a distant land, or when inhumation is environmentally unfeasible. In such cases the wishes of the family or the individual should be honored, and cremation should not be regarded as an evil or sinful act.

When the Christian is required to practice cremation by state law as is the case in parts of Japan, and could eventually be required in places like Singapore, Hong Kong or England, it is important that the funeral service clearly emphasize the hope of the believer in eternal life and the assurance of a future bodily resurrection. Perhaps, in places such as Singapore, Hong Kong and Japan, believers will need to establish their own crematoriums to prevent the intrusion of Buddhist idolatry which is so common at the ones currently in operation. A dignified burial of the remains would seem to be in order to symbolize the believer's hope of a future resurrection and to demonstrate respect for the body, God's creation.

Christian funerals need to return to simplicity, dignity and economy. They should be occasions when the focus is placed on faith, not elaborate display. Death provides special opportunities for ministry for which the church family must be properly prepared. A well organized bereavement committee can be of great assistance to the pastor and the sorrowing family.

Children need to be carefully instructed in a non-funeral setting about the issues of death and burial. A visit to a funeral home when a funeral is not in process has been found to be helpful to some. Children then can be introduced to the funeral environment without the emotions of the occasion, and explanation of the funeral process can go on much easier. Attendance at a particular funeral should be at the child's option after the aspects of the funeral are clearly explained.

The funeral, with all its sorrow and emotional pain, is an occasion of enormous opportunity for the Christian. In this most difficult time, the faith of the child of God can shine most brightly. Indeed, believers sorrow, but not as those who have no hope (1 Thess. 4:13). Only those whose faith is in the risen Christ can appropriate the confident statements of Paul such as "to die is gain" (Phil. 1:21), "to be with Christ . . . is far better" (v. 23), and "O death, where is thy sting? O grave, where is thy victory?" (1 Cor. 15:55, KJV).

Endnotes

PREFACE

[1] Ernest Morgan, ed. *A Manual of Death Education & Simple Burial* (Burnsville, NC: The Celo Press, 1975), p. 3.

CHAPTER 1

[1] Gen. 3:19; Rom. 5:12.

[2] Rom. 5:17-21; 1 Cor. 15:21-58.

[3] For a study of the methods and goals of burial excavation see, John J. Davis, "Excavation of Burials," *Benchmarks in Time and Culture*, ed. by Joel Drinkard, Gerald L. Mattingly, and J. Maxwell Miller (Atlanta: Scholar's Press, 1988), pp. 179-208.

[4] Paul Irion, "To Cremate or Not," *Concerning Death: A Practical Guide for the Living*, ed. by Earl A. Grollman (Boston: Beacon Press, 1974), p. 240.

[5] Donald Kent Smith, *Why Not Cremation?* (Philadelphia: Dorrance & Company, 1970), p. 42.

[6] *Ibid.*

[7] *Ibid.*

[8] James W. Fraser, *Cremation: Is It Christian?* (Neptune, N.J.: Loizeaux Brothers, 1965), p. 26.

[9] Jessica Mitford, *The American Way of Death* (New York: Simon & Schuster, 1963), p. 166.

[10] Quoted in *ibid.*, pp. 166-67

[11] Data supplied by The Cremation Association of North America.

[12] *Ibid.*

[13] *Ibid.*

[14] *Ibid.*

[15] Smith, Bucklin & Associates, Inc. Market research & Statistics Division in a report entitled, *Cremation: Projections to the Year 2000* (1988 Revisions) for the Cremation Association of North America, August 12, 1988.

[16] *Ibid.*

CHAPTER 2

[1] Paul E. Irion, *Cremation* (Philadelphia: Fortress Press, 1968), p.3.

[2] E. O. James, *Prehistoric Religion* (London: Thames & Hudson, 1957), p. 99.

[3] See A. Closs, "Cremation," *New Catholic Encyclopedia* IV (New York: McGraw-Hill Book Co., 1967), p. 440. Also see Jeanne Marie Lortie, "Cremation and the Catholic Church," *Homiletic and Pastoral Review*, 83 (1983), p. 54.

[4] Paul E. Irion, *Cremation*, p. 3.

[5] V. Gordon Childe, "Directional Changes in Funerary Practices During 50,000 Years," *Man*, 45 (Jan.-Feb. 1945), p. 14.

[6] Flora S. Kaplan, "Cremation," *The Encyclopedia Americana*, International Edition (Danbury, CT: Grolier Incorporated, 1981), p. 171.

[7] Nils-Gustaf Gejvall, "Cremations," *Science in Archaeology: A Survey of Progress and Research*, ed. by Don Brothwell and Eric Higgs (New York: Basic Books, 1963), p. 381.

[8] Nils-Gustaf Gejvall, "Cremations," p. 469.

[9] V. Gordon Childe, "Directional Changes in Funerary Practices During 50,000 Years," p. 14.

[10] Alfred Rush, *Death and Burial in Christian Antiquity* (Washington, D.C.: The Catholic University of America Press, 1941), p. 240.

[11] Robert W. Habenstein and William M. Lamers, *The History of American Funeral Directing*, rev. ed. (Milwaukee: Bulfin Printers, 1962), p. 31.

[12] Arthur D. Nock, "Cremation and Burial in the Roman Empire," *Harvard Theological Review*, 25 (1932), p. 327.

[13] See Joseph A. Callaway, "The Gezer Crematorium Re-examined," *Palestine Exploration Quarterly* (July-Dec., 1962), p. 117.

[14] This discovery is generally dated to the 14th or 13th centuries B.C. See David G. Mitten, "A New Look at Ancient Sardis," *Biblical Archaeologist*, 29 (May, 1966), p. 42. Ashes and bone fragments of a cremation were also found in a temple dating to the second century B.C. (*ibid.*, p. 61).

[15] Piotr A. Bienkowski, "Some Remarks on the Practice of Cremation in the Levant," *Levant*, 14 (1982), p. 82.

[16] *Ibid.*, pp. 84–85. Also see C.N. Johns, "Excavations at Pilgrims' Castle, 'Atlit (1933): Cremated Burials of Phoenician Origins," *Quarterly of the Department of Antiquities in Palestine*, 6 (1937), pp. 121–52.

[17] See E. Gaal, "The King Parrattarna Died and Was Cremated?" *Wirtschaft und Gesellschaft im Alten Vorderasien*, ed. by J. Harmatta and G. Komoroczy (Budapest: Akademiai Kiado, 1976), pp. 281–86.

[18] See G. M. A. Hanfmann, "The Fifth Campaign at Sardis (1962)," *Bulletin of the American Schools of Oriental Research*, 170 (1963), p. 55, footnote 62.

[19] See Piotr A. Bienkowski, "Some Remarks on the Practice of Cremation in the Levant," p. 80.

[20] Roland deVaux, *Ancient Israel* (London: Darton, Long-man and Todd, 1961), p. 57.

[21] Paul E. Irion, *Cremation*, p. 6. Also see Habenstein and Lamers, *The History of American Funeral Directing*, p. 31.

[22] Donna C. Kurtz and John Boardman, *Greek Burial Customs* (Ithaca, N.Y.: Cornell University Press, 1971), p. 26.

[23] See Paul E. Irion, *Cremation*, p. 6.

[24] Donna C. Kurtz and John Boardman, *Greek Burial Customs*, p. 36.

[25] J. M. C. Toynbee, *Death and Burial in the Roman World* (Ithaca, New York: Cornell University Press, 1971), p. 39.

[26] J. M. C. Toynbee, *Death and Burial in the Roman World*, p. 39. Also see A.W. Argyle, "The Historical Christian Attitude to Cremation," *The Hibbert Journal*, 57 (1958), p. 67.

[27] John J. Davis, "Areas F and K, The Fifth Campaign at

Tell Heshbon," *Andrews University Seminary Studies*, 16:1 (1978), p. 138.

[28] John Jamieson, "On the Origin of Cremation or the Burning of the Dead," *Transactions of the Royal Society of Edinburgh*, 8 (Edinburgh: Archibald Constable & Co.,1818), p. 117.

[29] See Robert W. Habenstein and William M. Lamers, *The History of American Funeral Directing*, p. 59.

[30] Flora S. Kaplan, "Cremation," p. 171.

[31] Arthur D. Nock, "Cremation and Burial in the Roman Empire," p. 358.

[32] J. M. C. Toynbee, *Death and Burial in the Roman World*, p. 41.

[33] Hilda Ellis, *The Road to Hel: A Study of the Conception of the Dead in Old Norse Literature* (London: Cambridge University Press, 1943), p. 8.

[34] Hilda Ellis, *The Road to Hel: A Study of the Conception of the Dead in Norse Literature*, p. 42. Also see Robert W. Habenstein and William M. Lamers, *The History of American Funeral Directing*, p. 29.

[35] Robert W. Habenstein and William M. Lamers, *The History of American Funeral Directing*, p. 78.

[36] Gale R. Owen, *Rites and Religions of the Anglo-Saxons* (London: David and Charles, 1981), p. 68.

[37] *Ibid.*, p. 88.

[38] Tadeusz Malinowski, "Funeral Customs of the Bronze and Iron Ages in Poland," *Archaeology* 16 (1963), p. 184.

[39] John Russell, "Cremation," *The American Ecclesiastical Review*, 153 (1965), p. 32.

[40] Flora S. Kaplan, "Cremation," p. 171. Also see E. O. James, *Prehistoric Religion*, p. 248.

[41] Flora S. Kaplan, "Cremation," p. 171.

[42] Mircea Eliade, *Patterns in Comparative Religion*, trans. by Rosemary Sheed (New York: Sheed & Ward, 1958), p. 250.

[43] Paul E. Irion, *Cremation*, p. 12.

[44] Flora S. Kaplan, "Cremation," p. 171.

[45] Nunzio J. Defoe, "Cremation and the Church in the Modern World," *Jurist*, 31 (1971), p. 638.

⁴⁶ *Cremation Cemeteries in Eastern Massachusetts* (Cambridge, MA: The Peabody Museum, 1968), p.5
⁴⁷ Flora S. Kaplan, "Cremation," pp. 171–72.
⁴⁸ *Des Carnis Resurrectione I.* Quoted in Alfred Rush, *Death and Burial in Christian Antiquity*, pp. 244–45.
⁴⁹ John F. McDonald, "Cremation," *Jurist*, 26 (1966), p. 206.

CHAPTER 3

¹ Bestram S. Puckle, *Funeral Customs: Their Origin and Development* (London: T. Weiner Laurie, 1926), p. 220.
² *Ibid.*, p. 222.
³ Donald Kent Smith, *Why Not Cremation?* p. 18.
⁴ Bestram S. Puckle, *Funeral Customs: Their Origin and Development*, p. 220.
⁵ Donald K. Smith, *Why Not Cremation?* p. 18.
⁶ P. Herbert Jones, ed. *Cremation in Great Britain* (London: The Pharos Press, 1945), p. 8.
⁷ William E. Phipps, "The Consuming Fire for Corpses," *Christian Century* (March 4, 1981), p. 221.
⁸ Bestram S. Puckle, *Funeral Customs: Their Origin and Development*, p. 222.
⁹ From a story in *The Observer*, Oct. 15, 1916, summarized in Bestram S. Puckle, *Funeral Customs: Their Origin and Development*, pp. 222–23.
¹⁰ Bestram S. Puckle, *Funeral Customs: Their Origin and Development*, p. 571.
¹¹ Jessica Mitford, *The American Way of Death*, p. 162.
¹² Bestram S. Puckle, *Funeral Customs: Their Origin and Development*, p. 220.
¹³ Donald K. Smith, *Why Not Cremation?*, pp. 16–37.
¹⁴ Robert W. Habenstein and William M. Lamers, *Funeral Customs the World Over* (Milwaukee: Bulfin Printers, 1962), p. 61.
¹⁵ William E. Phipps, "The Consuming Fire for Corpses," p. 221.
¹⁶ William S. Cook, "Cremation: From Ancient Cultures to Modern Usage," *Casket and Sunnyside*, 103:1 (Jan. 1973), p. 43.

[17] Robert W. Habenstein and William M. Lamers, *Funeral Customs the World Over*, pp. 59–60.

[18] Paul E. Irion, *Cremation*, p. 13.

[19] Jacqueline Wong, "Gifts for the Dead Keep Up with Times," *Straits Times* (Singapore, April 6, 1987), p. 32.

[20] *Ibid.*

[21] Robert W. Habenstein and William M. Lamers, *Funeral Customs the World Over*, p. 129.

[22] Paul E. Irion, *Cremation*, p. 12.

[23] William C. Cook, "Cremation: From Ancient Cultures to Modern Usage," p. 43.

[24] John N. Kane, *Famous First Facts*, 4th ed. (New York: H. W. Wilson Co., 1981), p. 208.

[25] Nunzio J. Defoe, "Cremation and the Church in the Modern World," p. 641.

[26] *Ibid.*

[27] Smith, Bucklin & Associates, *Cremation: Projections to Year 2000* (1988 Revisions).

[28] Ken Robinson, "Cremation: How it Began, Why it Spreads," *Casket and Sunnyside*, 101:1 (1971), p. 40

[29] Mark Canter, "Cremation Gains Favor At Last Goodbye," *The Bradenton Herald* (Sunday, Feb. 23, 1986), p. C-1.

[30] "Cheap Cremation Wins a Lease on Life," *Business Week* (August 12, 1972), pp. 31–31.

[31] Peggy McCarthy, "New Cremation Service Roils State's Funeral Directors," *New York Times* (Nov. 27, 1983), Section 23, p. 1.

[32] *Ibid.*

[33] Ken Robinson, "A Short History of Cremation," *Mortuary Management*, 58:3 (1971), p. 25.

[34] *The Cremationist* (April, May, June, 1985), p. 9.

[35] *Ibid.*

[36] J. Stephen Lansing, "A Balinese Faust," *Parabola*, 6 (1981), p. 7.

[37] Quoted in the *American Funeral Director* (May, 1975), p. 43.

[38] C. J. Polson, R. P. Brittain, T. K. Marshall, *The Disposal of the Dead*, second rev. ed. (Springfield, IL: Charles C. Thomas Publishing, 1962), p. 137.

³⁹ Nils-Gustaf Gejvall, "Cremations," p. 470.

⁴⁰ Jeanne Marie Lortie, "Cremation and the Catholic Church," p. 50.

⁴¹ M. B. Walsh, "Cremation (Moral Aspect)," *New Catholic Encyclopedia*, p. 441.

⁴² Jeanne Marie Lortie, "Cremation and the Catholic Church," p. 51.

⁴³ Nunzio J. Defoe, "Cremation and the Church in the Modern World," p. 641.

⁴⁴ Jeanne Marie Lortie, "Cremation and the Catholic Church," p. 52.

⁴⁵ "Funeral Rite in Japan Adapted to Cremation," *The Catholic Messenger*, 82 (May 28, 1964), p. 9.

⁴⁶ *Watchtower* (July 1, 1965), p. 416.

⁴⁷ Jeanne Pugh, "Altered Beliefs, Necessity, Change Attitudes on Cremation," *St. Petersburg Times* (June 23, 1979), p. 4.

⁴⁸ Cf. Gen. 23:19; 35:8; Deut. 34:6; 1 Kings 11:15; 22:37; and Ezek. 39:15.

⁴⁹ Abraham P. Block, *The Biblical and Historical Background of Jewish Customs and Ceremonies* (New York: KTAV Publishing House, Inc., 1980), p. 50. Also see Solomon B. Frehof, *Reform Jewish Practice and Its Rabbinic Background*, I (New York: KTAV Publishing House, 1976), p. 133.

⁵⁰ Jakob J. Kokotek, "The Jewish Attitude toward Cremation," *Pharos*, 28:4 (1962), p. 3.

⁵¹ Harry Rabinowitz, "Cremation," *Encyclopaedia Judaica* (New York: MacMillan Co., 1971), p. 1073.

⁵² Paul E. Irion, *Cremation*, p. 91.

CHAPTER 4

¹ Reuben Kashani, "Burial," *Encyclopedia Judaica* 4 (New York: Macmillan Co., 1971), p. 1516.

² Cf. 2 Sam. 21:9–10; 1 Kings 13:22; 14:11; 16:4; 2 Kings 9:35–37; Psa. 79:3; Jer. 7:33; 8:1–2; 16:4, 6; 22:19; Ezek. 29:5; Rev. 11:7–9.

³ 1 Sam. 31:11–13 and Amos 6:9–10. A reference to a cremation by the Moabites is found in Amos 2:1. All three of these passages are considered below in this chapter.

⁴ Psa. 13:3; Jer. 51:39; John 11:11–14; Acts 7:60; 1 Thess. 4:15.

⁵ Isa. 14:11; Ezek. 32:27.

⁶ For a complete study of Egyptian mummification practices and more detail on the embalming of Jacob and Joseph, see John J. Davis, *The Mummies of Egypt* (Winona Lake, IN: BMH Books, 1986).

⁷ 2 Sam. 3:30–31; Job 21:32–33; Eccl. 12:5; Jer. 9:17; Amos 5:16; Matt. 9:23.

⁸ The two exceptions have already been observed in footnote 3.

⁹ R. Laird Harris, "*Sarap*," *The Theological Wordbook of the Old Testament* 2, Harris, Archer, and Waltke, eds. (Chicago: Moody Press, 1980), p. 884. A list of verbs can be found in Aaron Pick, *The English and Hebrew Bible Student's Concordance* (Bible Study Classic, n.d.), p. 54.

¹⁰ Francis Brown, S. R. Driver and Charles A. Briggs, eds. *A Hebrew and English Lexicon of the Old Testament* (Oxford: The Clarendon Press, 1952), p. 976.

¹¹ 1 Sam. 31:12; 1 Kings 13:2; 2 Kings 23:16, 20; 2 Chron. 34:5; Isa. 47:14, Amos 2:1.

¹² William F. Albright, *Archaeology of Palestine*, 5th ed. (Baltimore: The Johns Hopkins Press, 1968), pp. 92–93.

¹³ *Ibid.*

¹⁴ Lawrence E. Stager and Samuel R. Wolff, "Child Sacrifice at Carthage—Religious Rite or Population Control?" *Biblical Archaeology Review* 10:1 (1984), pp. 31–51; Josette Elay, "The Relations Between Tyre and Carthage During the Persian Period," *Journal of the Ancient Near East Society of Columbia University* 13 (1981), pp. 15–29; and J. G. Pedley, "The Rite of Child Sacrifice at Carthage," *New Light on Ancient Carthage* (Ann Arbor: University of Michigan Press, 1980), pp. 1–11.

¹⁵ 2 Kings 17:17; Psa. 106:37–38; Isa. 57:5; Jer. 7:30–31; 19:5; 32:35; Ezek. 16:20–21.

¹⁶ 2 Kings 16:1–4; 2 Chron. 28:1–4.

¹⁷ 2 Kings 21:6; 2 Chron. 33:6.

¹⁸ For a discussion of the problem passage and the various views on it, see John J. Davis and John C. Whitcomb, *A*

History of Israel (Grand Rapids: Baker Book House, 1980), pp. 124–28.

[19] Such burials seemed to have been reserved for infamous persons (Josh. 8:29; 2 Sam. 18:17).

[20] Ex. 32:20; Deut. 7:25; 9:21; 12:3; 1 Kings 15:13; 2 Kings 10:26; 23:15; 1 Chron. 14:12; 2 Chron. 15:16.

[21] S. M. Houghton, "Earth to Earth: Burial Verses Cremation," *Bible League Quarterly* 323 (1980):374.

[22] Also note 2 Chron. 28:3; Isa. 30:33; Jer. 7:31; 19:5–6; 32:35. In all probability, it was in this valley that Manasseh offered his son as a human sacrifice (2 Kings 21:6; 2 Chron. 33:6).

[23] See R. Laird Harris, "*Sarap*," p. 884. It is interesting to observe that the parallel passage in 1 Chron. 10:12 omits the phrase, "and they burned him there."

[24] G. R. Driver, "A Hebrew Burial Custom," *Zeitschrift fur die alttestamentliche Wissenschaft* 66 (1954): 314–15.

[25] See John Mauchline, *I and II Samuel. New Century Bible* (Green, SC: The Attic Press, 1971), p. 193; Peter T. Ackroyd, *The First Book of Samuel. Cambridge Bible Commentary* (Cambridge: Cambridge University Press, 1971), p. 229.

[26] F. C. Cook, *I Samuel to Esther. The Bible Commentary* (Grand Rapids: Baker Book House, 1970), p. 71.

[27] S. Goldman, *Samuel* (London: The Soncino Press, 1969), p. 185. See also C. F. Keil and F. Delitzsch, *Biblical Commentary on the Books of Samuel* (Grand Rapids: Wm. B. Eerdmans Publishing Co., 1950), pp. 281–82; John P. Lange, *Samuel. Commentary on the Holy Scriptures* (Grand Rapids: Zondervan Publishing House, n.d.), p. 354 and Hans W. Hertzborg, *I and II Samuel: A Commentary* (Philadelphia: Westminster Press, 1964), p. 233.

[28] See C. F. Keil and F. Delitzsch, *The Twelve Minor Prophets* 1 (Grand Rapids: Wm. B. Eerdmans Publishing Co., 1949), p. 250.

[29] James W. Fraser, *Cremation: Is It Christian?* p. 14.

[30] William R. Harper, *Amos and Hosea. International Critical Commentary*, ed. by Driver, Plummer and Briggs (New York: Charles Scribner's Sons, 1905), p. 155; G. R. Driver, "A Hebrew Burial Custom," p. 315.

31 G. W. Ahlstrom, "King Josiah and the DWD of Amos 6:10," pp. 7-8.

32 See G.W. Ahlstrom, "King Josiah and the DWD of Amos 6:10," *Journal of Semitic Studies* 26:1 (1981), pp. 7-9; Keil and Delitzsch, *The Minor Prophets*, p. 302; Andre Neher, *Amos, Contribution of l'Etude du Prophetisme* (Paris: Librairie Philosophique J. Vrin, 1981), p. 105; and Henry McKeating, *The Books of Amos, Hosea, and Micah* (Cambridge: Cambridge University Press, 1971), p. 51.

33 W. Harold Mare, *I Corinthians. The Expositor's Bible Commentary*, ed. by Gaebelein, Boice, Tenny and Terpstra (Grand Rapids: Zondervan Publishing House, 1976), p. 268.

34 See for example, J.M. Fuller, *I Samuel-Esther. The Bible Commentary* (Grand Rapids: Baker Book House, 1971), p. 393; Otto Zockler, *Chronicles. Lange's Commentary on the Holy Scriptures* (Grand Rapids: Zondervan Publishing House, n.d.), p. 205; W. H. Bennett, *The Books of Chronicles. The Expositor's Bible* (London: Hodder and Stoughton, 1894), p. 360; John Bright, *Jeremiah. The Anchor Bible* (Garden City, NY: Doubleday and Co., 1965), pp. 214-15; and R.K. Harrison, *Jeremiah and Lamentations. Tyndale Old Testament Commentary* (Downers Grove, IL: InterVarsity Press, 1973), p. 146.

35 J. Barton Payne, *I and II Chronicles. The Wycliffe Bible Commentary*, ed. by Pfeiffer and Harrison (Chicago: Moody Press, 1962), p. 404; Zockler, *Chronicles*, p. 205 and Bennett, *The Books of Chronicles*, p. 360.

CHAPTER 5

1 William E. Phipps, "The Consuming Fire for Corpses," p. 221.

2 I am grateful to Mr. Ned Titus of Titus Funeral Home, Warsaw, Indiana, for this information.

3 Donald K. Smith, *Why Not Cremation?*, p. 2.

4 Donna Shaw, "A Tale of 47,000 Bodies, Final Resting Place Unknown," *The Philadelphia Inquirer*, 319:101 (Oct. 9, 1988), p. 1.

5 William E. Phipps, "The Consuming Fire for Corpses," p. 222.

⁶ "Funeral Rite in Japan Adapted to Cremation," p. 9.

⁷ Mary B. Comyns, *A Plea for Cremation* (Boston: Massachusetts Cremation Society, 1892), p. 20.

⁸ "Cremation," *Encyclopaedia Britannica*, 1946 ed. s.v., p. 665.

⁹ William E. Phipps, "The Consuming Fire for Corpses," p. 222. Also see Paul E. Irion, "To Cremate or Not," p. 247.

¹⁰ Richard L. Morgan, "Cremation," *The Christian Ministry* (May, 1984), p. 15.

¹¹ *Ibid.*, p. 14.

¹² Alan Wolfelt, *Death and Grief: A Guide for Clergy* (Muncie, IN: Accelerated Development, Inc., 1988), p. 149.

¹³ *Ibid.*, p. 123.

¹⁴ Kate Holliday and Jessica Mitford, "Two Conflicting Views on Cremation," *Good Housekeeping* (Feb. 1968), p. 76ff.

¹⁵ Everett W. MacNair, "Cremation or Burial," *Social Action* 25 (April, 1959), p. 15.

¹⁶ Donna Shaw, "A Tale of 47,000 Bodies," p. 1.

¹⁷ Mary B. Comyns, *A Plea for Cremation*, p. 14.

¹⁸ James W. Fraser, *Cremation: Is It Christian?* p. 25.

¹⁹ Everett W. MacNair, "Cremation or Burial," p. 14.

²⁰ Jill Morgan, ed. *This Was His Faith* (New York: Revell, 1952), pp. 253–54.

²¹ Richard L. Morgan, "Cremation," p. 14.

²² Thomas E. Spencer, "Cremation, An Expression of Life Style," *Journal of Individual Psychology* 28 (May 1973), pp. 60–66.

²³ Acts 5:6, 10; 8:1–2.

²⁴ Alfred Rush, *Death and Burial in Christian Antiquity* (Washington, D.C.: The Catholic University of America Press, 1941), p. 243.

²⁵ *Ibid.*

²⁶ Ignatius, *Epistula ad Romanos* quoted in Alfred Rush, *Death and Burial in Christian Antiquity*, p. 250.

²⁷ Tatian, *Oratio ad Graecos* 6,2, quoted in Alfred Rush, *Death and Burial in Christian Antiquity*, p. 251.

²⁸ Alfred Rush, *Death and Burial in Christian Antiquity*, p. 52.

[29] John Jamieson, "On the Origins of Cremation, or the Burning of the Dead," p. 88.

[30] *Contra Celsum*, VIII, 30. Quoted in Paul E. Irion, *Cremation*, p. 11.

[31] James W. Fraser, *Cremation: Is It Christian?* p. 15.

[32] Gregory Stricharchuk, "A Corpse is Gone, But Whose Death Was That Anyway?" *The Wall Street Journal* (Jan. 25, 1989), p. 1, 8.

[33] "Ashes of 9000 Are Found Dumped on the Ground," *The New York Times* (June 28, 1984), Sec. 1, p. 15.

[34] "Dear Abby," *The Warsaw Times-Union* (Oct. 3, 1988), p. 16. Abby's advice was, by the way, that the daughter should honor her father's wishes and allow the ashes to remain with his wife.

[35] John Johnson, "Macabre Tale of Scandal Rocks Cremation Industry," *The Fort Wayne Journal-Gazette* (Jan. 1, 1989), p. 9A.

[36] James W. Fraser, *Cremation: Is It Christian?* p. 20.

[37] John F. McDonald, "A Decade of Cremation in the Church," *The Clergy Review*, 60 (1978), p. 385.

CHAPTER 6

[1] Jessica Mitford, *The American Way of Death* (New York: Simon and Schuster, 1963).

[2] Ruth Mulvey Harmer, *The High Cost of Dying* (New York: Collier Books, 1973).

[3] Paul E. Irion, *The Funeral: Vestige or Value?* (Nashville: Abingdon Press, 1966).

[4] Alan D. Wolfelt, *Death and Grief: A Guide for Clergy* (Muncie, IN: Accelerated Development, Inc., 1988).

[5] Gale R. Owen, *Rites and Religions of the Anglo-Saxons*, p. 74.

[6] *Ibid.*, p. 79.

[7] Paul E. Irion, *The Funeral: Vestige or Value?* p. 65.

[8] Ernest Morgan, *A Manual of Death Education & Simple Burial* (Burnsville, NC: The Celo Press, 1975), p. 24.

[9] Richard L. Morgan, "Cremation," p. 14.

10 J. Ellwood, "Funerals for God's Glory," *Good News Broadcaster* (April 1985), p. 60.

11 Alan Wolfelt, *Death and Grief: A Guide for Clergy*, p. 124.

12 *Ibid.*

13 Donald K. Smith, *Why Not Cremation?* p. 7.

14 *Ibid.*, p. 60.

15 Richard L. Morgan, "Cremation," p. 15.

16 *Ibid.*

17 Charles A. Corr and John N. McNeil, *Adolescence and Death* (New York: Springer Publishing Company, 1986), p. 24

18 See Darlene E. McCown, "Funeral Attendance, Cremations, and Young Siblings," *Death Education* 8 (1984), p. 350.

19 J. Schowalter, "How Do Children and Funerals Mix?" *Journal of Pediatrics*, 89 (1976), pp. 139–42.

20 Darlene E. McCown, "Funeral Attendance, Cremation, and Young Siblings," p. 360.

21 *Ibid.*, p. 361.

Books

Ackroyd, Peter T. *The First Book of Samuel.* In *Cambridge Bible Commentary.* Edited by P. T. Ackroyd, A. R. C. Leaney, J. W. Packer. Cambridge: Cambridge University Press, 1971.

Albright, William F. *Archaeology of Palestine.* 5th ed. Baltimore: The Johns Hopkins Press, 1968.

Basevi, W. H. F. *The Burial of the Dead.* London: George Routledge & Sons, 1920.

Bendann, Effie. *Death Customs: An Analytical Study of Burial Rites.* New York: Alfred A. Knopf, 1930; reprint ed., Ann Arbor, MI: Gryphon Books, 1971.

Bennett, W. H. *The Books of Chronicles.* In *The Expositor's Bible.* Edited by W. Robert Nicholl. London: Hodder and Stoughton, 1894.

Bermingham, Edward J. *The Disposal of the Dead: A Plea for Cremation.* New York: Bermingham & Co., 1881.

Blackwood, Andrew W. *The Funeral.* Philadelphia: The Westminster Press, 1942.

Bloch, Abraham P. *The Biblical and Historical Background of Jewish Customs and Ceremonies.* New York: Ktav Publishing Inc., 1980.

Bowman, Leroy. *The American Funeral: A Study in Guilt, Extravagance, Sublimity.* Washington, D.C.: Public Affairs Press, 1959.

Bratt, John H. *Springboards for Discussion.* Contemporary Discussion Series. Grand Rapids: Baker Book House, 1970.

Bright, John. *Jeremiah.* In *The Anchor Bible.* Edited by W. F. Albright and D. N. Freedman. Garden City, NY: Doubleday and Co., 1965.

Brown, Charles. "The Environment of Disposal: The Exterior." In *Dying, Death and Disposal.* Edited by Gilbert Cope. London: S.P.C.K., 1970.

Chadwick, James R. *The Cremation of the Dead.* Boston: G. H. Ellis, 1905.

Choices to Make Now for the Future. Chicago: Cremation Association of North America, n.d.

Cobb, John Storer. *A Quarter-Century of Cremation in North America*. Boston: Knight & Millet, 1901.

Comyns, Mary B. *A Plea for Cremation*. Boston: Massachusetts Cremation Society, 1892.

Conway, Bertrand Louis. *Ethics and History of Cremation*. New York: Paulist, 1923.

Cook, F. C, ed. *I Samuel to Esther. The Bible Commentary*. Grand Rapids: Baker Book House, 1970.

Cope, Gilbert, ed. "Code of Cremation Practice of the Federation of British Cremation Authorities" Appendix in *Dying, Death and Disposal*. London: S.P.C.K., 1970.

Corr, Charles A., and McNeil, Joan N. *Adolescence and Death*. New York: Springer Publishing Co., 1986.

Covarrubias, Miguel. *Island of Bali*. New York: Alfred A. Knopf, 1937.

Cremation Cemetaries in Eastern Massachusetts. Cambridge, MA: The Peabody Museum, 1968.

Cremation Explained. Chicago: Cremation Association of North America, 1983.

Cremation Is Not The End . . . . Chicago: Cremation Association of North America, n.d.

Cremation Memorials. Chicago: Cremation Association of North America, n.d.

Cumont, Franz. *After Life in Roman Paganism*. New Haven, CT: Yale University Press, 1922.

Davidson, Glen W. *Understanding Mourning*. Minneapolis: Augsburg Publishing House, 1984.

Davies, J. G. ed. *Burial: A Dictionary of Liturgy and Worship*. New York: The MacMillan Co., 1972.

Davis, John J. *The Mummies of Egypt*. Winona Lake, IN: BMH Books, 1986.

_____. "Excavations of Burials." In *Benchmarks in Time and Culture*. Edited by Joel F. Drinkard, Gerald L. Mattingly, J. Maxwell Miller. Atlanta: Scholars Press, 1988.

_____, and Whitcomb, John C. *A History of Israel*. Grand Rapids: Baker Book House, 1980.

Dempsey, David. *The Way We Die: An Investigation of Death and Dying in America*. New York: McGraw Hill Book Co., 1975.

de Vaux, Roland. *Ancient Israel.* London: Darton, Longman and Todd, 1961.

Dincauze, Dena Ferran. *Cremation Cemeteries in Eastern Massachusetts.* Papers of the Peabody Museum of Archaeology and Ethnology, Harvard University, vol. 59. Cambridge, MA: Peabody Museum, 1968.

Dowd, Quincy L. *Funeral Management and Costs: A World Survey of Burial and Cremation.* Chicago: University of Chicago Press, 1922.

Eassie, William. *Cremation of the Dead: Its History and Bearings Upon Public Health.* London: Smith, Elder & Co., 1875.

Eliade, Mircea. *Patterns in Comparative Religion.* Translated by Rosemary Sheed. New York: Sheed & Ward, 1958.

Ellis, Hilda. *The Road to Hel: A Study of the Conception of the Dead in Old Norse Literature.* Cambridge: Cambridge University Press, 1943.

Erdmann, C. F. D. *Samuel.* Translated by Philip Schaff. In *Lange's Commentary on the Holy Scriptures.* Edited by John Peter Lange. Grand Rapids: Zondervan Publishing House, n.d.

Erichsen, Hugo. *The Cremation of the Dead.* Detroit: D. O. Haynes & Co., 1887.

Eusebius *Church History* 5. 1. 57–63.

Fraser, James W. *Cremation: Is It Christian?.* Neptune, NJ: Loizeaux Brothers, 1965.

Frazer, Persifor, Jr. *Merits of Cremation.* Philadelphia: American Academy of Political and Social Science, 1910.

Freehof, Solomon B. *Reform Jewish Practice and Its Rabbinic Background,* vol. 1. Hoboken, NJ: Ktav Publishing House, 1976.

Freeman, Albert C. *Antiquity of Cremation and Curious Funeral Customs.* London: Undertakers' Journal, 1909.

Fuller, J. M. *I Samuel-Esther.* In *The Bible Commentary.* Edited by F. C. Cook. Grand Rapids: Baker Book House, 1971.

Gaal, E. "'The King Parrattarna Died and Was Cremated'?" In *Wirtschaft und Gesellschaft im Alten Vorderasien.* Edited by J. Harmatta and G. Komoroczy. Budapest: Akademiai Kiado, 1976.

Gejvall, Nils-Gustaf. "Cremations." In *Science in Archaeology: A Survey of Progress and Research*, pp. 468–79. Edited by Don Brothwell and Eric Higgs. Foreword by Grahame Clark. New York: Basic Books, 1963; rev. and enl. ed., New York: Praeger Publishers, 1970.

Goldman, S. *Samuel*. London: The Soncino Press, 1969.

Gorer, G. *Death, Grief and Mourning*. New York: Doubleday, 1965.

Grey, Thomas C. *The Legal Enforcement of Morality*. Borzoi Books in Law and American Society. New York: Alfred A. Knopf, 1983.

Grollman, Earl A., ed. *Concerning Death: A Practical Guide for the Living*. Boston: Beacon Press, 1974.

Habenstein, Robert W., and Lamers, William M. *Funeral Customs the World Over*. Milwaukee: Bulfin Printers, 1974.

_____, and Lamers, William M. *The History of American Funeral Directing*. Rev. ed. Milwaukee: Bulfin Printers, 1962.

Harmer, Ruth M. *The High Cost of Dying*. New York: Cromwell-Collier Press, 1963.

Harper, William R. *Amos and Hosea*. In *International Critical Commentary*. Edited by Driver, Plummer and Briggs. New York: Charles Scribner's Sons, 1905.

Harrison, R. K. *Jeremiah and Lamentations*. In *Tyndale Old Testament Commentary* Downers Grove, IL: Inter-Varsity Press, 1973.

Henderson, Howard A. M. *Cremation: A Rational Method of Disposing of the Dead*. Cincinnati: G. P. Houston, 1890.

Hertzborg, Hans W. *I and II Samuel: A Commentary*. Philadelphia: Westminster Press, 1964.

Holder, William. *Cremation Versus Burial: An Appeal to Reason Against Prejudice*. Hudson, NY: A. Brown, 1891.

Huntington, Richard, and Metcalf, Peter. *Celebrations of Death: The Anthropology of Mortuary Ritual*. Cambridge, England: Cambridge University Press, 1979.

Irion, Paul E. *Cremation*. Philadelphia: Fortress Press, 1968.

_____. "To Cremate or Not." In *Concerning Death: A Practical Guide for the Living.*, pp. 239–52. Edited by Earl A. Grollman. Boston: Beacon Press, 1974.

_____. *The Funeral: Vestige or Value?* Nashville: Abingdon Press, 1966.

Jackson, Edgar N. *Telling a Child About Death.* New York: Hawthorn Books, Inc., 1965.

James, E. O. *Prehistoric Religion.* London: Thames & Hudson, 1957.

Jones, P. Herbert, and Noble, George A. *Cremation in Great Britain.* 3d ed. London: Pharos Press, 1945.

Kane, John Nathan. *Famous First Facts.* 4th ed., exp. and rev. New York: H. W. Wilson Co., 1981.

Keil, C. F., and Delitzsch, F. *Biblical Commentary on the Books of Samuel.* Grand Rapids: Wm. B. Eerdmans Publishing Co., 1950.

Kurtz, Donna C., and Boardman, John. *Greek Burial Customs.* Ithaca, NY: Cornell University Press, 1971.

Lange, Louis. *Church, Women and Cremation.* New York: U.S. Cremation Co., 1901.

McKeating, Henry. *The Books of Amos, Hosea, and Micah.* Cambridge: Cambridge University Press, 1971.

Mandelbaum, David G. "Social Uses of Funeral Rites." In *The Meaning of Death*, pp. 189–217. Edited by Herman Feifel. New York: McGraw-Hill Book Co., 1959.

Marble, John O. *Cremation in Its Sanitary Aspects.* Boston: Clapp, 1885.

Mare, W. Harold. *I Corinthians.* In *The Expositor's Bible Commentary*, vol. 10. Edited by Gaebelein, Boice, Tenny and Terpstra. Grand Rapdis: Zondervan Publishing House, 1976.

Mauchline, John, ed. *I and II Samuel. New Century Bible.* Greenwood, SC: The Attic Press, 1971.

Mertz, Barbara. *Red Land, Black Land.* New York: Dell Publishing Co., 1966.

Mitford, Jessica. *The American Way of Death.* New York: Simon & Schuster, 1963.

Morgan, Ernest, ed. *A Manual of Death Education and Simple Burial.* Burnsville, NC: Cleo Press, 1975.

Morgan, Jill, ed. *This Was His Faith.* New York: Revell, 1952.

Owen, Gale R. *Rites and Religions of the Anglo-Saxons.* London: David & Charles, 1981; Totowa, NJ: Barnes & Noble Books, 1981.

Payne, J. Barton. *I and II Chronicles.* In *The Wycliffe Bible*

Commentary. Edited by Pfeiffer and Harrison. Chicago: Moody Press, 1962.

Peirce, C. N. *Sanitary Disposal of the Dead.* Philadelphia: Philadelphia Cremation Society, 1891.

Pick, Aaron. *The English and Hebrew Student's Concordance.* Bible Study Classic, n.d.

Polson, C. J., and Marshall, T. K. *The Disposal of the Dead.* 3d ed. London: English Universities Press, 1975.

Puckle, Bertram S. *Funeral Customs: Their Origin and Development.* London: T. Weines Laurie, 1926.

Rush, Alfred C. *Death and Burial in Christian Antiquity.* Washington, D.C.: Catholic University Press, 1941.

Smith, Donald K. *Why Not Cremation.* Philadelphia: Dorrance & Co., 1970.

So You've Chosen Cremation. Chicago: Cremation Association of North America, n.d.

Stager. Lawrence E. "The Rite of Child Sacrifice at Carthage." In *New Light on Ancient Carthage.* Edited by John Griffiths Pedley. Ann Arbor, MI: University of Michigan Press, 1980.

Toll, N. P., ed. "Part II: The Necropolis." In *The Excavations at Dura-Europus Preliminary Report of the Ninth Season of Work 1935-36.* New Haven: Yale University Press, 1946.

Toynebee, J. M. C. *Death and Burial in the Roman World.* Ithaca, NY: Cornell University Press, 1971.

Wallace, Amy; Wallechinsky, David; and Wallace, Irving. *The Book of Lists #3.* New York: William Morrow and Co., 1983.

Wilson, Sir Arnold, and Hermann, Levy. *Burial Reform and Funeral Costs.* London: Oxford University Press, 1938.

Wass, Hannelore, and Corr, Charles A. *Childhood and Death.* New York: Hemisphere Publishing Corporation, 1984.

Zockler, Otto. *Chronicles–Esther.* Translated by James G. Murphy. In *Lange's Commentary on the Holy Scriptures.* Edited by John Peter Lange. Grand Rapids: Zondervan Publishing House, n.d.

Articles

Alger, Alexander. "The New (And More Convenient) American Way of Death." *Forbes* 158:10 (21 October 1996): 324-326.

"Ashes of 9,000 Are Found Dumped on the Ground." *New York Times* 28 (June 1984): Sec.1, A15.

Argyle, A. W. "The Historical Christian Attitude to Cremation." *The Hibbert Journal* 57 (1958): 67-71.

Becker, Marshall J. "Cremation Among the Lucanians." *American Journal of Archaeology* 86 (October 1982): 475-81.

Beer, John. "Consumed by Fire." *Theology* 86 (September 1983): 353-58.

Berg, William. "Cremations Continue to Increase." *Mortuary Management* 57:1 (January 1970): 18-19.

Bienkowski, Piotr A. "Some Remarks on the Practice of Cremation in the Levant." *Levant* 14 (1982): 80-89.

"The Body After Death." *American Funeral Director* (May 1975): 43.

Brown, Charles M. "Reducing the High Cost of Dying." *The Christian Century* (21 October 1936): 1391-93.

Brown, Frank E. "Violation of Sepulture in Palestine." *American Journal of Philology* 52 (1931):1-29.

Bruning, Nancy. "The Ecological Cost of Dying." *Garbage* 4:4 (July/Aug. 1992): 36-41.

Callaway, Joseph A. "Burials in Ancient Palestine: From the Stone Age to Abraham." *Biblical Archaeologist* 26 (September 1963): 74-91.

_____ "The Gezer Crematorium Re-Examined." *Palestine Exploration Quarterly* (July-December 1962): 104-17.

Canter, Mark. "Cremation Gains Favor as Last Goodbye." *The Bradenton* (FL) *Herald* (23 February 1986): Cl-C3.

Charles, C. F. "Increased Cremations Reported to American Cremation Association." *Casket & Sunnyside* 102:9 (September 1972): 23.

_____ "Increased Cremations Reported." *Casket & Sunnyside* 102:23 (1972): 23

"Cheap Cremation Wins a Lease on Life." *Business Week* (12 August 1972): 31, 32.

Childe, V. Gordon. "Directional Changes in Funerary Practices During 50,000 Years." *Man* 45 (January-February 1945): 13-19.

Connell, Francis J. "Problems of Professional People." *Liguorian* 45 (January 1951): 16-17.

Cook, S. A. "A Nazareth Inscription on the Violation of Tombs." *Palestine Exploration Quarterly* (April 1932): 85-87.

Cook, William S. "Cremation: From Ancient Cultures to Modern Use." *Casket & Sunnyside* 103:1 (January 1973): 42-44, 47.

'Cremation of Amputated Limbs.' *The Homiletic and Pastoral Review* 67 (1967): 794-95.

"Cremation: Permissible." *Time* (12 June 1964): 85.

Culican, William. "The Graves at Tell er-Reqeish." *Australian Journal of Biblical Archaeology I* (1973): 66-105.

Dahl, Edward C. "A Funeral Ministry to the Unchurched." *Pulpit Digest* 32 (1952): 11-16.

Daley, Evelyn. "Cremation: Presumptuous Proposal." *Catholic View* 26 (September 1962): 11-13

Davidson, Bill. "The High Cost of Dying." *Collier's* (19 May 1951): 13-19.

Davis, John J. "Areas F and K, The Fifth Campaign at Tell Heshbon." *Andrews University Seminary Studies* 16:1 (1978): 129-48.

Defoe, Nunzio J. "Cremation and the Church in the Modern World." *Jurist* 31 (Fall 1971): 638-46.

DeZulueta, F. "Violation of Sepulture in Palestine at the Beginning of the Christian Era." *Journal of Roman Studies* 22 (1932): 184-97.

A Dictionary of the Bible, 1903 ed., s.v. "Cremation," by Alfred Plummer.

Doty, Robert C. "Ban on Cremation Is Relaxed by Pope." *New York Times* (6 June 1964): 1.

Driver, G. R. "A Hebrew Burial Custom." *Zeitschrift fur die alttestamentliche Wissenschaft* 66 (1954): 314-15.

The Encyclopedia Americana, International Edition, 1981 ed., s.v. "Cremation," by Flora S. Kaplan.

Encyclopedia Britannica, 1946 ed., s.v. "Cremation."

Encyclopedia Judaica. s.v. "Burial," by Reuben Kashani.

Encyclopedia Judaica. s.v. "Cremation," by Harry Rabinowicz.

The Encyclopedia of the Lutheran Church. s.v. "Cremation," by Bruno Jordahn.

Encyclopaedia of Religion and Ethics. s.v. "Death and Disposal of the Dead," by E. Sidney Hartland et al.

Evans, J. Ellwood. "Funerals for God's Glory." *Good News Broadcaster* 43:4 (April 1985): 58-61.

Fitzgerald, Edward G. "Immediate Disposition-Fancy or Fact?" *Mortuary Management* 62:1 (January 1975): 11-15.

French, Hal W. "The Clergy and the Funeral Director: Complementary or Contrasting Perspectives. " *Death Studies* 9 (1985): 143-53.

Fulton, Robert L. "The Clergyman and the Funeral Director: A Study in Role Conflict." *Social Forces* 37 (1961): 317-23.

"Funeral Rite in Japan Adapted to Cremation." *The Catholic Messenger* 82 (May 28, 1964): 9.

Gadd, C. J. "The Spirit of Living Sacrifices in Tombs." *Iraq* 22 (1960): 51-58.

Gold, Gerald. "Wide Range of Funeral Prices Found Here in Consumer Study." *New York Times* (7 April 1974): 38.

Grinsell ' L. V. "Death and the After-Life." *Nature* 176 (October 1955): 809-12.

Gualtieri, Maurizio. "Cremation Among the Lucanians." *American Journal of Archaeology* 86 (October 1982): 475-79.

Hamilton, Kendall. "Final Resting Places: Will There Be Room for You?" *Newsweek* 129 (24 March 1997): 15.

Hanfmann, G. M. A. "The Fifth Campaign at Sardis (1962)." *Bulletin of the American Schools of Oriental Research* 170 (April 1963): 1-65.

Harbison, Janet. "New Patterns for American Funerals." *Presbyterian Life* (August 1, 1964): 8, 9, 27.

Harmer, Ruth Mulvey. "Funerals That Make Sense." *Modern Maturity* 17:3 (June-July 1974): 59-61.

Harris, Marlys. "The Final Payment." *Money* 26:9 (September 1997): 86-91.

Havemann, Ernest. "Are Funerals Barbaric?" *McCalls* (May 1956): 33, 96-97.

Heintel, Mel. "Some Thoughts on 'Catholic' Cremation." *The Priest* 43 (May 1987): 4-5.

Holliday, Kate, and Mitford, Jessica. "Two Conflicting Views on Cremation." *Good Housekeeping* (February 1968): 77.

"How Shall We Bury Our Dead?" *Zion's Watch Tower* (March 1888): 7-8.

Houghton, S. M. "Earth to Earth: Burial versus Cremation." *Bible League Quarterly* 323 (October-December 1980): 372-77.

The International Standard Bible Encyclopaedia. s.v. "Cremation," by George B. Eager.

The Interpreter's Dictionary of the Bible, s.v. "Burial," by William L. Reed.

"In Piles of Human Ashes, A Grim Fraud." *New York Times* (22 June 1997): 17.

"Is Cremation Proper for Christians?" *Watchtower* (1 July 1965): 416.

Jamieson, John. "On the Origin of Cremation, or the Burning of the Dead." *Transactions of the Royal Society of Edinburgh* 8 (1818): 83-292.

Johns, C. N. "Excavations at Pilgrims' Castle, Atlit (1933): Cremated Burials of Phoenician Origin." *Quarterly of the Department of Antiquities in Palestine* 6 (1937): 121-52.

The Jewish Encyclopedia. s.v. "Cremation," by Richard Gottheil.

"Keeping Funeral Costs in Line." *Changing Times* 45:6 (June 1991): 57-60.

Kelly, William H. "Cocopa Attitudes and Practices with Respect to Death and Mourning." *Southwestern Journal of Anthropology* 5 (1940): 151-64.

Kraeling, Carl H. "Christian Burial Urns?" *Biblical Archaeologist* 9 (February 1946): 16-20.

Labi, Nadya, et. al. "Cremation Nation." *Time* 150 (4 August 1997): 18.

Langer, Tom. "What the Church Teaches About Cremation." *Our Sunday Visitor* (November 1, 1987): 8-9.

Lansing, Stephen J. "A Balinese Faust." *Parabola* 6:4 (Fall 1981): 6-11.

Lortie, Jeanne Marie. "Cremation and the Catholic Church." *Homiletic and Pastoral Review* 83 (1983): 49-56.

MacNair, Everett W. "Cremation or Burial?" *Social Action* 25 (April 1959): 11-17.

Malinowski, Tadeusz. "Funeral Customs of the Bronze and Iron Ages in Poland." *Archaeology* 16 (1963): 183-86.

McCarthy, Peggy. "New Cremation Service Rolls State's Funeral Directors." *New York Times* (27 November 1983): Sec. 23, p. 1.

McCown, Darlene E. "Funeral Attendance, Cremation, and Young Siblings." *Death Education* 8 (1984): 349-63.

McDonald, John F. "Catholics and Cremation." *Tablet* 229 (1975): 542-43.

_____ "Cremation." *The Furrow* 22 (1971): 134-39.

_____ "Cremation." *Jurist* 26 (April 1966): 204-13.

_____ "A Decade of Cremation in the Church." *The Clergy Review* 160 (1975): 381-88.

Mitten, David Gordon. "A New Look at Ancient Sardis." *Biblical Archaeologist* 29 (May 1966): 38-68.

Morgan, Richard L. "Cremation." *Christian Ministry* 5 (May 1984): 13-15.

"A Move to Embalm 'Cremation Clubs.'" *Business Week* (21 September 1974): 89.

Murray, M. A. "Burial Customs and Beliefs in the Hereafter in Predynastic Egypt." *Journal of Egyptian Archaeology* 42 (1956): 86-96.

New Catholic Encyclopedia. s.v. "Cremation," by A. Closs.

New Catholic Encyclopedia. s.v. "Cremation (Moral Aspect)," by M. B. Walsh.

The New Encyclopaedia Britannica, 15th ed. s.v. "Embalming, Burial, and Cremation," by Ruth Mulvey Harmer.

Nock, Arthur Darby. "Cremation and Burial in the Roman Empire." *Harvard Theological Review* 25 (October 1932): 321-59.

Oglesby, William B. "The Resurrection and the Funeral." *Pastoral Psychology* 8:76 (November 1957): 11-16.

Palmeri, Christopher. "Funeral Prospects." *Forbes* 156:6 (11 September 1995): 45-46.

Phipps, William E. "The Consuming Fires for Corpse." *Christian Century* 98 (4 March 1981): 221-22.

_____ "Cremation is Gaining." *New York Times* (4 February 1981): Sec. 1, p. 23.

Pugh, Jeanne. "Altered Beliefs, Necessity Change Attitudes on Cremation." *St. Petersburg* (FL) *Times* (23 June 1979): Religion section, p. 1.

_____ "Cremation Practices Date Back to Neolithic Period." *St. Petersburg* (FL) *Times* (23 June 1979): Religion section, p. 4.

_____ "Recent Funeral Trends Revive an Ancient Church yard Custom." *St. Petersburg* (FL) *Times* (25 July 1981): Religion section, p. 6.

Ravo, Nick. "More Choose Cremation, Though Cost Can Rival Burial." *New York Times* 147 (12 October 1997): 10.

Riga, Peter J. "Cremation: Some Doubts." *Homiletic and Pastoral Review* 87 (November 1986): 61-64.

Robinson, Ken. "Cremation: How It Began. Why It Spreads," *Casket & Sunnyside* 101:1 (January 1971): 24, 40.

_____ "A Short History of Cremation," *Mortuary Management* 58:3 (March 1971): 25-26, 34.

Royce, James E. "The Church and Cremation Today." *The Priest* 42 (June 1986): 5.

Russell, John. "Cremation." *The American Ecclesiastical Review* 153 (1965): 30-38.

Shaw, Donna. "A Tale of 47,000 Bodies, Final Resting Place Unknown." *The Philadelphia Inquirer* (9 October 1988): 1, 26.

Spencer, Thomas E. "Cremation, an Expression of Lifestyle." *Journal of Individual Psychology* 28:1 (May 1973): 60-66.

Surlis, Paul. "Let Church Speak Out on Death, Dying." *National Catholic Reporter* 33:2 (10 Nov. 1996): 19-22.

Szanton, Andrew. "Changing Styles Bring Cremation Industry to Life." *American Demographics* 14:12 (December 1992): 25.

Taylor, Nick. "An Anxious Scattering of Ashes." *New York Times* 146 (23 August 1997): 23.

Tetzeli, Rick. "Death Trends From Des Moines and Beyond." *Fortune* 127:5 (8 March 1993): 12-15.

The Theological Wordbook of the Old Testament, 1980 ed., s.v. "Sarap" by R, Laird Harris.

Tunley, Roul. "Can You Afford to Die?" *The Saturday Evening Post* (17 June 1961): 24-25, 80-81.

Vecsey, George. "Flying for the Last Time." *New York Times* (9 September 1979): Sec. 21, p. 6.

Vendrely, Nancy. "Ashes to Ashes.'" *The Journal Gazette* (Fort Wayne, IN), (19 February, 1998): D1, 4.

The Westminster Dictionary of Worship, 1979 ed. s.v. "Burial 5. Baptist," by John E. Skoglund.

The Westminster Dictionary of Worship, 1979 ed. s.v. "Burial 6. Congregationalist," by Horton Davies.

The Westminster Dictionary of Worship, 1979 ed. s.v. "Burial 7. Jehovah's Witnesses," by A. Heley.

The Westminster Dictionary of Worship, 1979 ed. s.v. "Burial 8. Lutheran," by Alfred Niebergall.

The Westminster Dictionary of Worship, 1979 ed. s.v. "Burial 9. Methodist," by A. Raymond George.

The Westminster Dictionary of Worship, 1979 ed. s.v. "Burial 10. Old Catholic," by Kurt Pursch, A. E. Ruthy, and C. Tol.

The Westminster Dictionary of Worship, 1979 ed. s.v. "Burial 11. Plymouth Brethren," by F. F. Bruce.

Wolfelt, Alan D. "Bereavement and Children: An Historical Perspective." *Bereavement* (November/December 1987): 8.

_____ "Bereavement and Children: Questions, Funerals, and Explaining Religious Beliefs. " *Bereavement* 2:1 (January 1988): 16-17.

_____ "Essential Helping Qualities." *Bereavement* 2:3 (March/April 1988): 8, 36.

_____ "The Funeral Ritual: Repression vs. Expression." *Mortuary Management* 67:5 (May 1980): 11, 13.

_____ "Men in Grief: A Naturally Complicated Experience." *Bereavement* 2:5 (June 1988): 31-32.

_____ "On Being a Compassionate Friend." *Thanatos* 7:3 (1982): 18.

_____ "Reconciliation Needs of the Mourner: Reworking a Critical Concept in Caring for the Bereaved." *Thanatos* 13:1 (1988): 6-10.

_____ "Sarah's Grief Continues: Understanding Regressive Behaviors in Bereaved Children." *Bereavement* 2:5 (June 1988): 17-18, 38.

_____ "Understanding Common Patterns of Avoiding Grief." *Thanatos* 12:2 (1987): 2-5.

_____ "Understanding an Apparent Lack of Feelings in the Bereaved Child." *Bereavement* 2:4 (May 1988): 17-18, 38.

_____ "We are the Compassionate Friends." *Thanatos* 6:12 (1981): 12-13.

Wong, Jacqueline. "Gifts for the Dead Keep Up with Times." *Straits Times* (Singapore) (6 April 1987): 32.

The Zondervan Pictorial Encyclopedia of the Bible. s.v. "Burial," by W. H. Mare.